IN EVERY
# SEASON

## TORN CURTAIN PUBLISHING
Auckland, New Zealand
www.torncurtainpublishing.com

ISBN Softcover 978-1-991299-64-2
ISBN EPub 978-1-991299-65-9

This book is not intended as a substitute for professional counselling or medical advice.

Cover art by Violetta Khabanets. Used with permission.

Typeset in Millar Banner, Raleway and Minion

Cataloguing in Publishing Data

Title: In Every Season: Rediscovering God's Hope Through Pain, Burnout and Shattered Faith
Author: Rachel Rerekura-Tamaiva
Subjects: Burnout, mental health, christian ministry and leadership, church planting, poetry, inspirational.

A copy of this title is held at the National Library of New Zealand.

# IN EVERY SEASON

REDISCOVERING GOD'S HOPE THROUGH PAIN,
BURNOUT AND SHATTERED FAITH

RACHEL REREKURA-TAMAIVA

For Tumanako — always faithfully at my
side through the best and worst.

# Contents

| | |
|---|---|
| *Author's Note* | *1* |
| *Introduction* | 5 |
| AUTUMN | 9 |
| WINTER | 31 |
| SPRING | 61 |
| SUMMER | 87 |
| *Epilogue* | *115* |
| *Acknowledgements* | *121* |
| *About the Author* | *125* |

# Author's Note

This book is a personal journey of spiritual, emotional and physical change framed through the lens of natural seasons and through the eyes of a woman. The unravelling of my life and involvement in a church ministry context led me through a pathway of deep transformation, reflection and learning, God uncovering new things in every season that needed my attention and needed His touch. This book is not a tale of instant recovery but a story of hope during my wrestling, my doubt, physical pain and rupturing of faith, a story that led to moments of change and a path to renewal. As women, I want us to be able to speak and share about the ways God has carried us but be honest about the deep valleys, dark nights, and questioning along the way.

Sister, in sharing these words, my prayer is that you would see God's hope and hand through my journey and reflect on the same in your own life, no matter where you are in your story. I invite you to reflect on the rhythms in your life as you engage in the reflection questions at the end of each season and give yourself time to sit in the learning, in the uncomfortable truths and in solidarity with other women around you whom you know are experiencing similar things.

This book is not written from bitterness but from healing and deep revelation. This is the book that I wished I had and the learnings I wish I had read about as I walked through the seasons of burnout and pain as a woman, a mother, and church ministry leader.

Thank you for choosing to go on this journey with me.

*The thing about seasons is that despite their unpredictability, they still uphold a pattern, a timeframe, a structure. We know, without a doubt, that each season follows another. We know that each season will change, and something different will eventually come. We know that after the unsettling coldness and darkness of autumn and winter is the long-awaited hope and warmth of spring and summer. We know that deep below the surface lies the possibility of growth, freedom, and new life.*

*We know that a season is not forever.*

# Introduction

In 2020, at the age of thirty-seven, I found myself in excruciating physical and emotional pain, experiencing clinical burnout. This was the catalyst for a faith crisis, leading me to question everything I had ever known about Jesus and this life I thought I was living for Him. Today, I sit in a place of reflection and hope as I pen my story. It is a story filled with the twists and turns of Christian ministry life, and documents my slow journey towards healing and understanding. I am not an expert. I am no theologian, nor am I a renowned church leader. Rather, I am a woman, a mother, a writer, and a lover of God and people. The pages that follow contain some of my thoughts and learnings during a season of burnout and pain. I hope they will encourage you, challenge you, and ultimately help you to draw closer to God in His infinite and gracious love.

As a young family with two children, my husband and I felt called to travel across the Tasman Sea from our home country of Aotearoa, New Zealand, to Australia to support the pioneering of a new church. Our hearts were ablaze with anticipation. The newness of the mission excited and motivated us, and the opportunity to experience a different way of life and a 'new normal' seemed like a great adventure. As we explored this new terrain, both spiritually and physically, we laboured, we sacrificed, and we loved—oh, how we loved!

We had another child in Australia, and as our family expanded to five, our ministry also grew exponentially. God brought beautiful people and families into our sphere, and we soon began to see incredible transformation, healing and restoration in hearts and families as we gathered, expanded, and released creativity into the church community. God was doing incredible work, and we were joyous in our praise. The fires in our hearts were burning—as was the midnight oil as we strived to get everything done. At some point, however, there was a shift, and our frenetic, exciting, industrious lives began to reveal cracks in our spiritual and emotional foundations. I always assumed that I could do all things through Christ, who gives me strength (Philippians 4:13). It turns out that even though in Christ I *can* do all things—the things He has in mind for me—that doesn't mean I need to do *all the things*. I was in the midst of trying to do 'all the things' when my world began to crumble.

During my wild season of change, God unravelled some important things within me. I asked Him to, and He kindly obliged—even though we both knew how much it would hurt. In the process, I had to relinquish who I was before—to step away from being known as a certain type of person who acted in expected ways. With all the sparkles dulled, the platform stripped away and the fancy frosting melted, God exposed the core of me. The dirty, grimy, messy core that lay underneath all the rest. And it wasn't a quick wash and dry cycle either. It was a slow unravelling, one layer at a time, one thing revealing another. Yet, through it all, the Holy Spirit offered hope and change whilst also reminding me He was with me every single messy step of the way.

Alongside this surrender of self, I was also forced to surrender everything I knew about God and His love for me. I had to bring before Him all the things I had been led to believe—and all the ways I had subsequently led others. I soon realised that my pain was impacted by all of the influences, opinions and experiences around me, as well as the motivations within me. I was taken to ground zero and back to the start. Back to nothing. The scaffolding had been well and truly dismantled, and it revealed a building that could not hold itself up. To build a more solid foundation, the old one first had to come down.

This book is something I wish I had when the pain was unbearable, and fear and adrenaline kept me awake long into the night. When I felt compelled to withdraw to dark places, what I needed most was insight, truth, compassion, and hope. This book provides space to speak about the different lessons God taught me in each season. In the same gentle and truthful way that He spoke to me, I want to give you the space to ask questions and flesh out the complexities of ministry, being a woman and a mum, and navigating friendship and faith in our middle years. I hope, too, that you will hear my heart. I love God, I love His church, and my faith has been strengthened (and challenged) through this journey. I have come to love the Bride of Christ through the sharing of an encouraging word, a meal offered to someone in need, a robust theology discussion, and the intricate differences among my three children. God is everywhere and working in everything. I have been continually amazed by His kindness, even amidst the pain. That God would allow us space to work with Him through our questions, doubts, pride, joy, miracles and change is more than I can fathom. And He doesn't rush us. He is gracious enough to wait, and He always leaves the door open.

'Clinical burnout' seems to be a cultural buzzword today, so I do not use the term lightly. For me, it represented a diagnosed condition characterised by hormone imbalances, exhaustion, and emotional fatigue, which caused me to withdraw from everyday activities and relationships and reduced my capacity to cope due to severe pain and mental stress. Maybe you find yourself in a similar space, dealing with the pain and confusion of this condition. Perhaps you are just starting on your ministry journey and you want to avoid treading that same path. I cannot promise you that. While I have no idea what God will illuminate to you on the way, I can share my journey with you—the lament, the hope and the lessons that God has mercifully shared with me. Although the things I have learned are personal to me, by conversing with friends and other women, I have realised that much of it is also a shared experience. The details may be different, but the journey is universal; as women, we have crossed over the same path and walked the same stepping stones many times over.

I hope you know you have a sister in Christ right here who loves God but has wrestled with faith, relationships, and the Christian ideals that were embedded deep within my psyche. I have struggled with doubt, theology, the church, and the part we are all given to play in the Body of Christ. I have asked big questions and have allowed myself time and space to wander through the change that has accompanied the different seasons of this journey. And I am still learning.

I hope this book encourages you and helps you to feel loved and understood, knowing that there is no shame in searching and seeking. So, take your time. Find solace in our shared experience, take a breath, and journey with me through the seasons.

PART ONE

# AUTUMN

*Trees lose their leaves in autumn to prepare for the coming winter. When the snow, heavy and bitter, enters the atmosphere, the tree is not fully laden and unable to cope; rather, it is equipped to bear the load that is likely to come. The tree changes colour as it soaks in the goodness of the leaves before they drop, knowing instinctively that it will need this goodness in the months ahead. Autumn, though unsettling and confusing, was a time of change and preparation for me—a necessary exposing and unravelling to brace for the winter that lay before me.*

# Autumn: Shift

When things start to unravel
When the growth starts to wither
And the vibrancy starts to fade

Things that were once full of life
Become stripped of their life
The pulsating activity
The crackle of new birth
Suddenly dulled

As leaves falter and waver in the wind
The trees bare themselves of colour
Bracing for the season to come
Not quite aware of the life
That waits on the other side

Autumn
As the end
But much more so
as the beginning

# Into the Struggle

In the autumn of 2020, as the natural seasons began to change, a change also began to take place in my physical body. When I started to experience crippling headaches, I had no idea what was to come. At first, they were short-lived but excruciating, stopping me in my tracks. Having not experienced this type of pain before, I knew there was something taking place in my body that needed attention, though I tried to make the best of it and hoped it would go away. Over the following six months, however, the headaches continued to worsen and take a toll, becoming longer, more frequent, and incredibly painful. Pain clinics, tests, neurologists and scans turned up no answers. During this time, I was forced to work from my bed, lying down as I struggled to hold my head up without pain. As I navigated COVID-19 lockdowns, organised life with our three children, and remained heavily involved in church ministry, my health deteriorated. I could no longer stand to hang out the washing, attend social engagements, or sit on my children's bed to say goodnight. In fact, this once-simple act now required me to crawl up the stairs and down the hall to reach their bedroom before immediately laying my head on their pillow. I was in pain every day, yet these physical signals were still not enough to make me stop.

I remember leading a Sunday team one morning when straight after communicating a welcome and singing a song, I had to rush into the kids' space to lie down because my headache was so severe. That was the sacrifice, right? I was doing God's work, I had faith, I had joy in every circumstance, and my body needed to come into alignment with my spirit. Well, that's how I justified it at the time. I was carrying so much pride, and I was so stubborn in my efforts to keep going that I was unwilling to address the cost of continuing in this pattern and refusing to take my body seriously. I had neglected to listen to Holy Spirit's promptings about the areas in my life that needed to be addressed and continued instead to turn a blind eye.

I didn't know it then, but I was already in the early stages of clinical burnout. My adrenal fatigue was impacting my hormones, and it was these messed-up hormones that produced the headaches that were literally bringing me to my knees. My Cortisol was flying way too high, and my Progesterone levels were scraping along the ground. I had been running on adrenaline for so long, trying to do everything and be everything to everyone, that my body just started to crumble. It took months to identify the cause. Months of trying to be a hero and continuing to do it all. It wasn't until I became emotionally withdrawn and unable to cope because of the pain that I began to pay attention to my body. It's almost funny how tightly we continue to hold onto our control even in the midst of overwhelming difficulty or pain. We are driven by the fear of how things might turn out if we drop any of the balls we are carrying—even the balls we are not supposed to be carrying at all.

During this season of physical change, as I became dull and numb emotionally and physically, a spiritual change began within me. I knew inherently that my spirit and body were linked and that the open door I allowed God to walk through was about to turn every part of me upside down. I was laid bare like a tree that loses its leaves and becomes exposed to the elements. As my mind and spirit began this metamorphosis, my physical symptoms continued to decline. It felt like my body had known this was coming, and I had been holding my breath for so long. This was the exhale—a painful, slow and revealing breath out. It was time to start listening.

# The Invitation

The first part of my unravelling started with an open door. Before the headaches, I had an ache in my spirit that some things were not right in my life. I remember having the most vivid dream as I entered the new year: God's glory demolishing and consuming everything in its midst as it hurtled towards me. God was showing me in that dream that though everything around me might crumble—all the familiar structures and environments I relied upon—my family and I would be okay. We were protected. This reassurance enabled me to trust God through the proceeding few years, and I thought of it often. Following this dream, I invited God to come and shake things up, strip away the parts of me that didn't serve His purposes, and access the areas I had been keeping to myself. As I read Psalm 73:17 in The Passion Translation, I realised this was my prayer, too:

> *"But then one day I was brought into the sanctuaries of God,*
> *and in the light of glory, my distorted perspective vanished."*

So, I prayed that as I entered into the glory of God's presence, He would make known all of my distorted perspectives and the areas that required change, growth, and His loving hand.

I spent so long trying to do all the things to manage such a busy life, desperately wanting others to believe I had it all together. And for a long time, I think I really believed I did. Yet, despite the big smiles and warm hugs as we were leading, serving, and pastoring others, I was perpetuating a false narrative that being a follower of Christ meant I could do it *all*. Not just the 'all' that He had designed for me, but all of everything. This seemed to be the popular narrative in the world around me—the narrative that led to 'success'. *I am a woman! I can do all things! I can work and play and mother and have a never-ending pot of gold-plated energy and thrive. Woohoo!* And guess what? People loved that about me! *I* loved that about me! *Gosh, aren't I doing so much and achieving so many things?!* Yet, this only fuelled my inaccurate belief that if I made a mistake, it would all fall apart. So, I held everything tighter and worked even harder.

Somewhere along the way, it had become about me—about approval, affirmation, and achievement. I took pride in the way I handled my busy-working-mum-church-leader life. I wore it like a badge. I remember one of my colleagues asking me how I did it all. At one point, I would get up at 5 a.m., catch the 6:10 a.m. train into the city, work a full day in a government policy role, catch the train home, do the school or daycare pickup, cook dinner, then head out to a meeting, family group or music practice of some sort two to three times a week. Sundays were church days, which often involved multiple services throughout the day with the kids in tow. My response to my awed friends was, "It's all God," but in my heart, I was actually thinking, *I know, aren't I awesome!*

Since my husband and I served alongside each other and on church staff at various times, much of our lives was one big juggle. We were faithful pillars who were ready to serve. We always said yes! But in doing this, I unknowingly sowed into my life (and the lives of others) a false narrative. I saw success in worldly terms: numbers, recognition, results, achievements, frenetic schedules, and rushing from one thing to the next. And by believing that narrative and focusing on meeting the expectations of others, I lost sight of the specific purposes God had for my life.

After seven years in church ministry, the rose-coloured glasses were long gone and my golden hour was coming to an end. The busyness and stress of juggling church ministry with my intense work and family commitments was finally starting to catch up with me. I started questioning in earnest the reasons why we were living this way and what foundation our lives were built on. I wondered about the structure and roles within our ministry environment, including accountability, governance, and future direction. I pondered our commitment to missions and the wider community. *Were we actually living out the purpose of God's church or just constantly in the throes of building something bigger and better for ourselves?* I thought a lot about where our true loyalties lay and whether our faithfulness to those around us had stopped us from being faithful and obedient to Christ. I tried to look ahead to my children's future—their discipleship and faith and what fount they would draw from in order to remain whole and healthy. Ultimately, I questioned everything about my relationship with Christ, and as I waded through the muddy waters of what was man-made and what was from Him, I began to wonder: *Who am I really following?*

You might be questioning your own church's ministry environment—their religious practices, connection to community, a sense of 'spiritual obligation', and financial integrity. As a strong and independent woman, I was capable and tenacious—grabbing onto everything, saying yes too many times over, and being proud of the way I could handle it all. But the life I had built around me was just a dull reflection of the promises and purposes God had mapped out for me. Yes, my life made an impact—I loved others, and I was busy doing godly things. However, I realised I was merely dancing around the edges of the life God had intended for me. I needed to go deeper.

Friend,
God has to unravel
He has to allow us to reveal our core
Unwrapping the layers
The history
Insecurity
Pain

He makes His way to the depths
And we need Him there

He's the only One gentle enough to take us through
To hold us
To lead us
To be patient with us

This journey to the deep requires all of us
And it requires our Creator
Creator and created
This journey is not walked alone

# Broken Pieces

As the autumn barrenness settled in, my life felt as scattered as the leaves on the ground—a myriad of colours in varying forms of decomposition. As someone who enjoys structure, planning, strategy, and knowing what's next, this was unnerving. We get very good at curating our lives, don't we? I enjoy strengthening processes to ensure a streamlined approach, forming good communication channels, and fixing things that are not working effectively. I can look at something and see its faults, then come up with solutions for change. This can be both a blessing and a curse, and I am still trying to determine if this is a natural talent or a learned behaviour. I have had to work very hard to be a flexible person (this might be an oxymoron!) and to be open to things changing at the last minute. The quickest way to learn this is to become a parent, where pivoting and navigating change become second nature. Someone needs to go to the toilet or can't find their shoes the very moment we are rushing out the door, or an unwell child puts an end to long-awaited social plans. I have been known to get frustrated and perhaps a little anxious when things do not go according to plan (apologies to my family for how this has played out). There seems to be so much pressure to have it all together, and without realising it, our lives can become a pattern of forced rhythms, practised to perfection to ensure efficiency.

I will be the first to tell you the value of a good plan. There is nothing wrong with an organised calendar, a family planner, good time management, and clear goals. These are all good things. But perfection is impossible to maintain when we live in an ever-changing world filled with the unexpected and the unwelcome, the bad and the good. Why, then, do we continue to maintain this façade before our God of mystery—the God who allows the unpredictability of life and is the only One who knows how the days of our lives will play out?

Many of us have become so rigid in our plans and structures that we do not allow ourselves the time, understanding and space to absorb the unpredictable realities of humanity or the changes that occur as we transition from one season to the next. Friend, whatever is happening and wherever you have found yourself today, let me just speak hope to you for a minute. Wherever you are right now is okay. Whatever mess you find yourself in is okay. Allow yourself to take a breath, welcome the unexpected, and accept the mess into your life. Give yourself permission to just be. Give yourself permission to rest.

As a social worker, I often recommend the following box breathing technique to clients I work with who are experiencing overwhelm, anxiety, panic, and stress, and I have used it myself many times when feeling anxious or rushed.

*Take a good, long, deep breath.*

*Inhale for four seconds, hold for four seconds, exhale*
*for another four seconds, and rest for four seconds.*
*Then repeat.*

Slow, deep and simple breathing allows the right flow of oxygen, reduces the body's Cortisol levels, and gives our brain time to relieve the stress caused by our fight, flight or freeze response. It creates the time and space to breathe (literally), take a moment, and rest.

Friend, you might be on the verge of something uncomfortable today. Perhaps it's a place you know God is taking you while holding your hand. Maybe it's a place that will bring some hard truths and difficult learning. You may feel the change of seasons beginning to take shape in preparation for something different—the shedding of unhelpful thinking, the unrest in your spirit, your foundations shaking as the summer sun sets and makes way for an upcoming transformational change. You might need some courage in this moment. You might need the spark of hope—to know that there is daybreak somewhere. You might hear the whisper of the Holy Spirit but feel fearful of what lies ahead. Know that you are not alone, you are loved, and the road ahead could be the most valuable journey of your life. There might be things that you know will need to change or need to be broken, and the pain and fallout will be immeasurably difficult. Friend, I am so sorry that your journey might include pain and uncertainty. Please know that God's love for you is never unsure—it is as certain as the rising sun every morning! God has space to hold you in this next season as you walk the path you know you need to tread. As you do what you know you need to do, I pray for God's peace and nearness.

If you have just heard some incredible news or had some amazing successes, I am so proud of you. You are allowed to feel joy. Shout it from the rooftops or celebrate silently—either is okay. I am right here with you, celebrating your successes and the way you have overcome obstacles to be where you are today. Perhaps you are now deciding what's next, making important decisions, and determining how to navigate this success. You might feel the tug of pride or self-admiration, or hear the whisper of self-doubt that creeps in all too often when things seem to go our way. As you take the next step forward, I pray God provides His wisdom and humility as He propels you forward into your purpose and all that lies in store. I pray that there is a future ahead of you that is alive with hope and expectations. I thank Jesus for these successes in your life, and I hope this is you living out some of your wildest, God-given dreams.

Conversely, as you read this, you might feel like crumpling in a heap. You are experiencing the lowest of lows, the most difficult of things, and you are walking a very hard road. You are feeling broken and empty, questioning if God is with you and known to you. Maybe you are facing an impossible health challenge and cannot see God in the midst of it, or you feel drained by the effort of supporting others through their own struggles and pain. Friend, I lament for you. I weep with you. It is okay to be where you are right now. It is okay to be confused, hurting, doubting, grieving. These things do not disqualify you from a life of fulfilment or joy. They do not cut you off from a loving God, even if you cannot feel Him or have trouble believing Him right now. Believe me, I know this mess. My mess may speak my language and reflect my life's history and patterns, but it is still a mess.

Thankfully, God does not shy away from our mess. He does not throw His hands up and walk away. He does the opposite—He takes our burdens from us, carrying them on His shoulders, and then He redeems us and our stories. We no longer have to live up to society's standards of perfection—our plans, our schedules, our curated lives. Whilst we might be 'showing up' for others, we do not need to show up for God. He shows up for us.

Friend, your mess is safe in this space. And it is safe with God. This doesn't mean that there won't be changes or that God won't prompt you towards something new or different. But for today, God is okay with your mess. He understands it, and He has compassion for it. He is ready for you to be honest with Him and lay it all out on the table. He held me in my weakness and brokenness, and He will hold you, too.

If our Creator God, in all His greatness, can love humanity even with all our messy imperfections, maybe it's time for us to accept them also. Maybe it's time to invite God into the unstructured and messy areas of our lives, asking Him to interrupt our careful plans to breathe new life and hope. Friend, I implore you to let God into your mess today as you read, weep, hope, and laugh. Allow yourself to be seen by a God who is for you and who is patient and kind. Unfurl those hands, unwrap your heart, open your eyes, and let Him see all of it.

# Ask for Help

We are never quite complete whilst we are here on earth—we are human after all! Thankfully, God doesn't stop caring for us. He doesn't stop moulding and shaping us. And this learning process continues— all our life long! Until heaven and earth collide in our own personal journeys, we can rest assured that God is still working in us. As my physical body engaged in this seasonal change and unravelling, I found that every new revelation from God exposed yet another layer I had to work through. I was forced to go deeper and deeper, uncovering and digging in the dirt. Still, my heart was always open and willing despite the stretch and discomfort. God was requiring more of me, and there was no going back now.

As I began to crumble in the initial stages of this transformation process, I felt so much shame. The person I was becoming in this autumn season—struggling with social connections, emotionally disengaged, and unable to see things through or feel the joy around me—was not me. *How, then, could I be honest about where I was at, and whom could I trust with the shame and disappointment I felt at letting myself and others down?* My pride made me keep this to myself for longer than I should have. But God worked through this with me, too. He knows that sharing our struggles with people we trust is an important part of the healing journey.

Receiving encouragement when I divulged my deepest and darkest fears provided valuable insight into my dearest relationships. I still teetered on the brink of shame and fear at times, concerned at what even my closest friends thought of me. I allowed them to be honest with me in their struggles, but I still felt I shouldn't be truly honest about mine. In truth, trusting my heart with a few beautiful people and seeking their wise counsel created stronger bonds, transparent communication, and a place of rest and encouragement for me in the messiest of times. I asked for help and support from those around me whom I knew I could trust with my whole self—even the worst parts—and I am so glad I did. My husband and I also met with some very special, older and more experienced people along the way, who created a trustworthy space for us to process all the pain, changes and questions together. It was a great relief to garner wisdom and compassion from others who have walked the same road, and the time we spent together was priceless.

One of the best decisions I made throughout this process was to seek professional help. Initially, I sought out a Christian counsellor who had experience working with ministry leaders, and I was able to wade through all my questions and theological wonderings that had been sparked during this initial season of change. These conversations allowed me to safely examine the source of my frustration and concern whilst identifying the desires and promptings of the Holy Spirit that I had long been ignoring. These sessions were challenging but insightful, helping me to make sense of some of the changes happening in my spirit.

Additionally, after seeking medical help and getting nowhere with my physical symptoms, I turned to a naturopath, whose wisdom created a breakthrough in understanding what was happening physically. This newfound knowledge finally helped me to navigate the treatment that was required for my body to bring physiological stability. I still treasure the support and understanding I received, and I'm so thankful for the discernment that came from their years of experience. In all honesty, I do not know where I would be or what treatment I would be relying on if I had not gone down this road. Please know, however, that this path of treatment is mine alone and does not mirror everyone's journey. My goal here is not to recommend a specific treatment but to speak of the strength that comes from sharing your story and seeking support, both relationally and professionally.

Through my work, I was also privileged to have regular professional supervision with a psychologist. This allowed me to understand how everything I had journeyed through up to this point had an impact on my work, ministry, relationships, and mind. Each of these professional connections has been such a gift to me, offering great insight, experience, and understanding—and challenging me when needed. If I had continued to be stubborn and allowed pride to stop me from seeking help, I believe things would look very different now. Still, even though I am thankful for the support I received, it took courage and bravery to overcome my hesitations and share my story. I had to be willing to listen to other people's wisdom and guidance, willing to make some hard choices, and above all, willing to change.

The support I received also enabled me to fully understand and identify my fleshly desires and the impact they had on my relationship and intimacy with Christ. I was able to gather insight into the workings of my mind and heart, my unique self and personality traits, and my innermost needs and desires. I was given honest advice about the new habits, patterns and rhythms that I needed to adopt into my life and routines. I began to practice starving my desires, focusing instead on intimacy with Christ and spiritual wholeness. This was, and still is, a journey. The fleshly desires that bring us momentary relief, comfort and satisfaction often feel good. They can even sometimes be disguised as faithful endeavours. The desire for acknowledgement or approval can sit under the guise of overt generosity, servant-heartedness, or having a yes attitude. The pursuit of health and fitness can disguise a need for control and perfection. Coveting things we don't have and constantly wanting more can hide behind a good work ethic, financial blessing, and career success. The platform can make a way for pride and selfish ambition. These are often traits that we observe in others but miss in ourselves.

It is not weak to ask for support. For me, it was necessary. It takes humility to be honest about our struggles, but bringing dark things into the light, seeking godly wisdom, and involving professionals where we need them are all acts of strength. God speaks in many different ways, and sometimes we hear Him through the words and wisdom of others. So, ask for help. Get support.

Through wise counsel and a lot of heart work, I began to question and unravel my motivations, intentions, and desires—even the things that felt justified, good, and well-intentioned. It was terrifying to expose some of the darkness that was hidden in the depths, lurking in the shadows behind the spotlight. As God helped me to turn the spotlight towards my own heart, it was messy. It still is. I often revert to my default sinful nature, like we all do. But God, in His kindness, keeps bringing me close, shining a light and reminding me of His goodness and the freedom that comes when we choose Him. I know I have His power within me, and I can use it to shift my thoughts, my countenance, my words, and my actions.

My journey with trained professionals has not been separate from God. My mental health, physical health and spiritual health are not individual pieces of a puzzle that I can simply pop into a box and deal with in isolation. There is no part of my being that God is not part of or interested in. I truly believe that, as humans, we have been created for a relationship with Christ and that all parts of our being are designed for such a purpose. I sought help from Christian professionals because I knew that wholeness and healing would not come from personal insight, knowledge, or medication alone. These are all helpful—in some cases, they can even be critical to our healing—but they do not make us whole. Insight, knowledge, strategies, medication and tools offer us deeper understanding, help us determine a new pathway ahead, and allow our bodies and nervous system space to breathe and rest. But separate from God, these things cannot bring wholeness. We were designed for a relationship with Him, and only He can bring full healing and restoration.

Proverbs 11:14 tells us that there is safety in a multitude of counsellors. We were not meant to battle difficult things on our own. It does not make us any less holy to seek help. It does not make us weak or unfaithful. God expected us to live our lives in community, to be sharpened by one another. What a gift it is that God has allowed us to understand human behaviour as much as we do and that incredibly gifted humans choose to study and learn how to support us in knowing ourselves better. Having the opportunity to sit with godly, intelligent, spirit-filled professionals, who understood me and offered wisdom without judgement, has been one of the greatest blessings of this journey.

# Start with Surrender

At some point in the unravelling, I had to let go. I had to surrender everything into the hands of Christ and lay it all down at the foot of the cross. Believe me, I know how this sounds. "Just give it to God, you just have to lay it all down" are phrases many of us have heard before, and this act of surrender is often offered as a one-stop stepping stone to redemption and healing. It's easy to say, but how do we actually do it?

It can feel like a cop-out when someone offers wise words but doesn't know how to practically help us.

Matthew 11:28 offers an invitation to go towards God with the things that weigh heavy on our hearts, our minds, and our physical bodies. This verse promises us that if we align ourselves with Him—if we come to God with our burdens and trust Him with the hard, heavy and worrisome things in our lives—there is rest. Sometimes, we need others to help us shape our surrender by encouraging or challenging us, offering professional insight, or lifting us up in prayer. In this process, there is an acknowledgement that God is far more able to carry the weight than we are, and we can trust Him to hold it. This sometimes also involves entrusting our stories and struggles to mentors, counsellors, friends, or family.

I am reminded of hikes I have taken where I have carried a heavy pack—some of the contents are my own, and some are from others. It slows me down, and it sometimes throws me off balance. When I reach a place to rest and place my pack on the ground, I feel a sense of relief. I can move with agility, I feel lighter (literally), and the pain subsides. I may still have sore shoulders in the coming days—a reminder of the journey I have been on—but in that moment of laying down, there is freedom. In my autumn season, I had a choice to make. I could keep going *my* way, allowing life and vitality to slowly seep away whilst holding onto stubbornness and pride. I could uphold my façade and believe that everything I had created was good and faithful and true. I could continue making decisions out of fear and religious obligation. Or I could choose to surrender my pack, listening and responding in obedience to His loving voice and wisdom—even through the discomfort.

Unhealthy habits, thought processes, beliefs and theology were all embedded in my heart. I was so confused and had trouble discerning healthy from unhealthy, truth from lie. I knew I could not pick and choose—if I was going to surrender, it needed to be everything. My future (and the future of my husband, children, and marriage), my dreams and purposes, my relationships, my hurt, my history, my expectations and disappointment—I needed to surrender it all willingly and allow God to examine every area. Amid the pain of letting go, I had to choose to stay soft-hearted towards Him and keep trusting Him. I had to be willing to lose everything.

When we surrender our lives to God, we are choosing to take our hands off the steering wheel, trusting that the direction in which He chooses to take us will lead us on a road of discovery that we would never have found ourselves. But surrender is hard; it is a sacrifice. To surrender is to let go of the grip we have on something and freely give it away. Just as a tree slowly allows for the shedding and dropping of leaves in preparation for winter, surrender creates an open space for God to come in and transform our lives. It can seem impossible to let go when the things we are gripping onto so tightly are our life's work, friendships, goals, and all we have known. It can feel scary to surrender and choose to step into a dark and unknown place. Yet, Jeremiah 29:13 tells us that we will find God if we seek Him with our whole heart—all of it. And when we seek Him, He will transform our distorted thoughts and desires. He will bring healing where there is pain, He will bring joy where there is mourning, and He will bring hope when it feels that all hope is lost. And when we find Him, there is nothing He cannot and will not do to bring restoration to our lives.

Friend, the journey starts with surrender. It starts when we lay things down and open our hearts and lives in openness and humility. I had to be okay to go wherever God would take me. I knew that full surrender meant undoing. I knew that it meant change. I knew it meant stepping out of the comfortable and familiar into the unknown—trusting that God would hold me and lead me. I knew it meant denying myself and choosing to follow Him, no matter what, and allowing God into thoughts and spaces I had not previously been willing to lose. Ultimately, I knew I had to lose the life I had built so that I might find Jesus all over again.

# Autumn Reflection

Invite God into your inner world today.

🌹 What areas of your life are you holding onto tightly? Is there anything you are trying to control and do *your* way?

_____

_____

_____

_____

_____

_____

_____

_____

_____

_____

🌹 What messes have you not yet been able to allow God to touch, speak into, and heal?

_____

_____

_____

_____

_____

_____

_____

_____

_____

_____

_____

🌹 Who could you go to for help? What is stopping you from accessing that support?

_____

_____

_____

_____

_____

_____

_____

_____

_____

_____

🌹 What does surrender look like for you?

_____

_____

_____

_____

_____

_____

_____

_____

_____

_____

🌹 How could you give God all of your heart?

_____

_____

_____

_____

_____

_____

_____

_____

_____

_____

_____

_____

*If you are experiencing distress, harmful thinking, or are in the midst of a mental health crisis, I urge you to seek immediate professional or medical help. Speaking up and accessing necessary support from trusted individuals will support your journey of understanding and wholeness. Please know you are valuable, you are loved, and your health and well-being are undeniably important. You are not alone x*

PART TWO

# WINTER

*Winter brings a new season of isolation and hardship: biting winds, incessant rain, and a barren horizon. Sometimes, the dark winter nights can feel endless and the cold, unrelenting. Whilst winter seasons are an inevitable part of our lives, they can be unforgiving and harsh, complete with unexpected storms and challenges. Numbly, we trudge through the exposed landscape, lacking life and vitality. Yet even as winter bites, nature rests and restores itself below the surface, waiting for the right time to emerge. Winter is necessary, as are the seasons of darkness we must walk through. Though it's often invisible, we can trust change is taking place slowly in the unseen places.*

# Winter: Wait

Where the cracks are fully formed
And the dry, cold earth crunches underfoot
Where the elements are relentless
Unable to see new life
Unable to breathe yet in the hope of future growth
The changing and shifting below the surface
Unseen and unheard
Almost in disbelief
The darkness overflows
And light seems so far away
Pain penetrates and hope retreats
We wait in the dimness
Of dusk
And hope that in return
There will also be dawn

# In the Dark

The next three years would be tumultuous, confusing, and painful. As I began to understand my body and embark on a journey of physical healing, my progress was unpredictable. I sought natural processes to support healthy adrenal function and level my hormones, but my body reacted in all sorts of ways. I was balancing a confusing concoction of natural herbs, food scheduling, external appointments, and rest, and it took a long time to find a rhythm that was manageable and effective. There was a lot of trial and error regarding doses, food testing, exercise, and sleep strategies. Sometimes, I would vomit from the pain. On other days, I would eat to ease the pain and vomit from the food. Due to financial constraints, I could not just stop working as recommended, and since we had left most of our family and close friends behind in New Zealand, we were often on our own. During this season, I experienced a flurry of headaches and extreme exhaustion as we struggled to understand what was actually working and battled to survive.

During one holiday with my family, we headed to the local market. I typically love shopping for locally made products, and my children delight in the colourful displays of jewellery, handmade goods, and food treats, so I was determined to have fun despite my crippling headache. I remember bending my head down at every stall because relief only came when my head was down. I pretended to look closely at every item on offer when, in fact, I simply craved relief from the pain. I'm quite sure every vendor thought I was an intensely interested customer! Sadly, our expedition didn't last very long, and I had to head back to our holiday accommodation to lie down. Our fun night out was abruptly halted, much to my frustration and despair.

When I started to experience short bursts of relief from the pain, I would have anxiety about its unpredictability. Fearful of its return, I worried how long I might last without it. The pain was so great that it dictated my emotions, further triggering my Cortisol levels and the symptoms that led me to this point. As I drove to work in the morning, I would feel the effects of the Cortisol slowly rolling through my body— shoulder and neck tightness and tingling, a racing heart, and shallow breathing. Subsequently, I would arrive at work already wondering how bad the day would get and how debilitating the pain was going to be. Specific worship songs brought me such solace during this time—I would sing them, cry through them, and sometimes just sit silently listening because I did not have the words or energy to do more. These were moments of such sweet intimacy with Christ, though I did not receive the miracle or instant healing I was asking for. The rollercoaster of that season seemed relentless.

Amid the pain, however, God was opening my eyes. It wasn't until my competence was crippled that I could see my need to look competent to others. It wasn't until my health pulled me from the platform that I could see my unhealthy focus on people's affirmation and applause. It wasn't until I had anonymity that I realised how badly I wanted to be known. It wasn't until my heart and emotions were in disarray that I could understand the fact that God had created me to be an emotional being and connect with the emotions of others. It wasn't until I was weak that I could see all the ways I was broken. It wasn't until I was brought to my knees in pain and desperation, offering God all of me, that I was open to seeing what He had been trying to show me all along—His unfathomable, all-encompassing, forgiving, merciful love.

I am reminded of Joseph (whose story we read in the book of Genesis) stripped of his pride, his title as the 'favourite son', and his man-made identity and thrown, quite literally, into a season of pain, rejection, and slavery. Yet, during this barren winter season, God shaped him and began to establish a new identity within him—an identity that would bring restoration, wholeness, and purpose. Just like Joseph, we can put our hope in the God who forms us through the fire and uses the winter of our lives to transform our stories.

During this time, God spoke to me about the things I had missed and the words I had failed to hear, and He was gracious enough to share much-needed wisdom. Autumn and winter may have been my undoing, but they would lead to something far more beautiful.

It's a holy mess
This theology of mine
A tangle of truth and mistake
Good intentions or justified sin
I don't know where to let you in

How much of my reflection
Is mere counterfeit?
Fed by the drive for perfection
Excellence, class
The foundation I thought was concrete
Is actually just glass

And I wrestle
And repeat
My head above the mess
For a moment it is clear
And I think I know
Only to stumble again instead

Where are you
And who is your church?
How do I wade through the mess
To love you first?

# Room for Grief

To lament is to demonstrate sorrow, grief, and regret. Sometimes described as wailing or mourning aloud, it is an action, a verb. Ecclesiastes chapter three tells us there is a time for everything, including lament. God's Word gives us permission to actively express our sadness and grief.

Our tears spill over what was lost
The opportunities we have missed
The disappointment of dreams not realised
The salt streaming down our faces, healing our wounds
Releasing our pain

Our soul unravels and our eyes give way to rivers
Torrents that hold nothing back
And we move through this ocean of desperation
To a moment of peace
Like a hand outstretched to pull us out.

And somehow, in that river of despair lies a new hope
With every drop that falls to the earth, an opportunity
For forgiveness
For courage
For letting go

A window of clarity that makes its way to our heart

Lament is not something I had been taught or thought much about, nor was it a term I had often heard mentioned in church. It did not provide uplifting content for Sunday messages, and it wasn't included in any of our 'New Christian' courses. Yet, as my physical body began to heal, I found that I was experiencing immense sadness and loss. A loss of dreams and outcomes. A loss of relationship. A loss of health and capacity. A loss of intimacy with others. I hadn't realised how much grief and loss I carried with me that I had not allowed myself to express. I began to wonder: *Is it appropriate to lament if I know and have faith in a loving and powerful God? Can I hold joy in my heart and also lament for things lost and broken?*

Part of my journey has been to understand that leaving room for lament is not only healthy, it is biblical. Since the Bible displays God's understanding of the human condition—the challenges and losses we face, the hopelessness we feel, and the injustices we see in our world—it is full of examples of healthy lament, even from Jesus. Many components impact our capacity for lament: our trauma, cultural background, family relationships, social acceptability, toxic positivity, and even our theology. There are many obstacles to experiencing raw vulnerability with God and with others. Sometimes, they are even disguised as strength and courage. Yet, when we hold back our lament, our grief and emotions can inhibit the beautiful and transformative work that God does through this process of full surrender.

Part of making space for God is acknowledging our emotions before Him. The myriad of emotions that God gifted us with are all distinctly important and acceptable to Him. An emotion in itself is not a bad thing. Emotions help us to express ourselves, share our feelings with others, and release what is inside of us. They are helpful clues about what is happening in our heads and hearts. How to respond to them in a healthy way is often our biggest struggle. Rather than brushing them away, it is important to identify the 'why' behind them. *Why am I feeling frustrated? Why doesn't this situation feel right? Why do I feel anger and a sense of injustice in this? Why is my heart experiencing this kind of sadness?*

Loss, a part of the human experience that often causes grief and sadness, can be so easily skimmed over. We often think of grief in terms of loss of life, the various stages of grief, life trauma, or losing something major. We do not always think of grief in terms of loss of friendship, dreams, capabilities, or control. We may not want to personally acknowledge the loss of these things or even share them with others.

Biblical lament was an active and public display of emotion and often included wailing and tearing of clothes. It was an accepted part of people's lives—not shunned, hidden, or repressed. But in the churches I have attended (and in much of the West), this is not expected behaviour at all. Wailing was rare (and judged), and I certainly never saw anyone rip their clothing in grief and despair. As a leader, I reserved my best, happiest, friendliest and healthiest behaviour for Sundays so I could demonstrate God's joy to others. And I am not alone. Rather than showing people our vulnerability, we have learned how to show people our strength and attempts at perfection. Why? Because we want them to see that God is good and we are blessed. However, God's blessing does not equal the absence of troubles or tears (John 16:33). As God's children, made in His image, we have been created with the capacity to feel a myriad of different emotions. Even though they all have their place, we do not always permit ourselves to express our most complicated or intense feelings due to guilt, shame, and unhelpful religious expectations.

As leaders, we need to consider how we can and should be allowed to express our emotions within the church environment. Do we feel comfortable bringing difficult emotions like confusion, grief, anxiety and regret into the church building or does it feel safer to deal with them behind closed doors? Do we allow ourselves the freedom to express our lament, or must we constantly portray wholeness, purpose and clarity to be a fount of encouragement to others? Do we give ourselves the space to respond to the intimacy, healing and all-encompassing arms of the Holy Spirit during our Sunday services, or are we too busy responding to the needs of others to notice what He is up to? Will we be judged as disqualified if we fall apart during one of our services, or will we experience the love and acceptance of the people we are called to serve?

I remember walking into a new church environment during my season of healing. Without knowing anyone, I stood at the back and wept a river of tears. I was not known, but I felt loved. I felt that my tears were not only acceptable here, but they were acceptable to God. I allowed myself to feel and express the grief of walking away from the church we had been a part of and given our lives to, and the relationships we built over that time. I grieved the journey I was on and the way things had turned out. I grieved lost connections. I grieved the physical and emotional pain I was still experiencing. Putting into words the echo of my heart, I finally let myself lament.

Until I was a leader in church ministry, I never understood the grief I would feel when people left the church. I was not mad about it; I just loved them, and then they were gone. Sometimes, we knew why; other times, we didn't. Sometimes, we saw them before they left; other times, we didn't. Mostly, we did not retain much contact, and catch-ups were few and far between. I understand. I have been there. But, on reflection, I don't think I did much to care for them as they left. I didn't fully consider how they might be feeling about leaving, or appreciate the loss they must have felt in their hearts. I didn't recognise that they were on personal journeys with God, just as I was. All too quickly, we pivoted back to our vision for the church and the people who faithfully came with us. I regret not keeping in touch with those people—friends we still love but are now disconnected from. I'm sad because even though they may have needed us during that time of transition, we were too busy carrying out our mission—ready to engage with those who might walk in the door. I'm sorry that those who left may have felt isolated, because I know how loneliness feels.

I don't think I ever slowed down enough to verbalise the sadness I felt when people I truly loved disconnected from our church family. Instead, I pushed my feelings aside and kept moving, as we often do. There was always a next step—new people to meet and teams to encourage. I now know I didn't leave myself space to lament the loss I felt, and it impacted me more than I realised.

I encourage you, then, to keep loving the people who move on, move away, and choose to no longer be a part of your community. Lament the gap that they leave in your lives. Give it words and airtime with God. Don't leave space for bitterness or animosity—no matter what others might say. Instead, permit yourself to grieve the loss. Find a safe space to express your sadness and look for trusted people to share this burden with you. And, friend, if you can continue connecting with people you love who have chosen to leave, please do. Please choose to engage with them even through discomfort and awkwardness. If they are not ready, that's okay. If they are not safe people for you and you need to create a boundary, please do so. But just because someone doesn't attend our church anymore, that doesn't mean we cannot hold space for them in our lives.

I regret the number of times I have heard church members being likened to objects that can be 'poached' or 'stolen' by other pastors or congregations or witnessed frustration from leaders when their 'sheep' choose to move to another pasture or pastor. As leaders, we might spend years sowing into, loving and serving someone only for them to move elsewhere, and the reality is it hurts! There may be times when we need to have hard conversations and challenge unwise motivations or rash emotional decisions, but it is important to remember that people ultimately make their own choices and decisions. There may be a myriad of reasons, emotions and relationships that contribute to someone leaving a church, and we may just have to accept that things have not worked out the way we thought they would. This is all part of our life journey, and people are still precious. I am not speaking here about betrayal, moral mishaps, or abuse, and I am cognisant that each situation can be individually complex. But even if you do not understand why someone in your church decides or feels called by God to move into another ministry or community, bless them as they go. We can never truly know what is happening in someone's heart or spirit, what God is prompting them towards, or the truths He is revealing to them. Our job is simply to pray for them and trust that God is with them and working in their lives.

People do not belong to anyone aside from God, and it does not benefit the Kingdom of God if we get mad at another church or pastor because some of our flock moved on—even if it causes us emotional hurt or damages our ego in the process. Rather, we should want the best for them and desire that they should flourish—wherever they are. We can and should, therefore, continue to love the people who are dear to us outside of the parameters of our church family. They may still desire the connection as much as we do.

I also urge you to lament the dreams that have yet to be, or will likely never be, realised. We tend to have a picture in our minds of the things we will achieve and the path our lives will take. Yet, over and over, God demonstrates His faithfulness as we walk through painful and unexpected circumstances, and amid the pain and uncertainty, He shows us His faithfulness. Yet, even as we cling to Him for dear life in the middle of our storms, we don't often permit ourselves to acknowledge the mistakes, the disappointments, or the loss of our dreams.

The story of Lot's wife in Genesis 19 serves as a warning not to look back as we move forward with our lives. Coveting the worldly things she was leaving behind, Lot's wife disobeyed God's direction to keep her eyes ahead and was subsequently turned into a pillar of salt. Jesus also warns us that if we have our hand to the plough and look back, we are not fit for the Kingdom (Luke 9:62). But in Matthew 23:37-39 and Luke 13:34-35, we read that Jesus laments over Jerusalem. Lament is not the same as coveting the past. Lament does not stop us from moving forward. Lament is a powerful expression of our grief. And while He doesn't want us to linger there, grief itself is a gift from God. When we lament, we can trust God will meet us in the dark, hard, and lonely places. He understands our grief for we are made in His image, and He created us with the ability to feel and express this emotion. To ignore grief and lament is to ignore a part of ourselves designed and approved by God. Jesus did not allow His lament to stop Him from the work He had been created to do, but He did allow room for it in His life.

Friend, it is healthy for you to lament the sorrow and grief you are experiencing. Lament lost relationships, the death of loved ones, unexpected changes, and the injustices you see around you. Lament is undignified; it is supposed to be messy and loud, and you will find relief in your tears as you let your body do its job. And whether you weep publicly or privately, know that you are seen by God, who keeps track of all your sorrows and collects your tears in His bottle (Psalm 56:8).

So, take some time to speak aloud your grief. Write out your lament. Freely express the pain, sadness and despair you once felt or are feeling now. God promises to be with you through every season, and you can trust Him with the things you care about because He cares for you.

# Tribe Over Team

Real, honest human connection is like water to the soul. The central focus of Christianity is a belief in a relational God, a triune being existing in love and connection. I have found that women tend to have an inherent ache for deep, authentic friendship. We desire to be part of a community of people with different personalities, backgrounds, gifts, and goals, who know us from top to bottom—down to the smallest nuance. We long to find a safe space to bring our questions about life, relationships, faith, and friendship. We crave relationships that are not motivated by ambition or selfish desires but are simply enriching, valuable, and fun! So why do I hear so many women in their thirties and forties exclaim that friendship is so hard to find?

Most people, at some point in their lives, take an inventory of their friendships and feel deflated, disappointed, left out, or not good enough. It's par for the course. By comparing our lives with others and seeing evidence of what we might be missing out on—the playgroups we weren't invited to, the elite clique we are not quite cool enough to join, that tribe of women who seem unshakeable in their friendship and are always out having fun—our tiny handful of friends can suddenly feel inadequate.

As a young family, we left our home country, friends and family behind to support the planting of a new church. We very quickly lost contact with many friends back home because we were so focused on building our lives around our new church family. I am so grateful for those who stayed in touch over that time, checking in even when I was too busy trying to change the world. I thank God they stuck with me through FaceTime and text messages across the ocean!

As our ministry expanded over the years, we met the strongest and most incredible people. We shared delicious meals and had so much fun together. Still, many of our relationships during this season were missional. We were focused on connecting people to the fabric of the church—making them feel welcome, leading them in a team, and helping them take the next step in their faith journey. These are not bad things! Yet, we found ourselves feeling very alone at times. There is complexity in creating safe, honest and enriching relationships whilst leading a ministry. It takes wisdom and discernment to walk the fine line between allowing our fragile human selves to be seen—mistakes and all—whilst also setting clear boundaries and taking personal steps towards spiritual maturity.

As a result of our circumstances, our church had become our family. When we felt it was time to move on from that environment, we didn't realise we were leaving many of these relationships behind, too. We lost our tribe and family twice. Amid a season of parenting young children and spiritual upheaval, we felt lost. It was an unexpected loss, and it left us in a hard place.

Whilst pain is universal, vulnerability in sharing that pain with others is not. We live in a culture that is eager to shed light on humanity's struggles with mental and physical health and relationships whilst becoming, at the same time, more and more focused on portraying one's best self. There is a tension between being vulnerable and sharing too much, confessing that you're not okay whilst still maintaining some sense of decorum and social etiquette, and being truly authentic while also carefully handpicking moments to share with others. There are either too many filters or no filters at all—it's all so confusing.

I often ponder how the early church was described in the Bible, specifically in Acts chapter two. This was a community of believers in which resources were shared, meals were enjoyed together, and people worshipped, prayed, and lived in community. Many of us know that we don't truly know a person until we live with them. Perhaps you stayed with your in-laws and picked up nuances you hadn't noticed before. Maybe it wasn't until you lived in a dorm room with another student, camped in a tent with friends or holidayed with another family that you understood them on a deeper level—the way they operate, the things that frustrate them, the desires they yearn for. There are intimate details you cannot know about a person until you are living in close proximity to them. Yet, it is here where pain is shared and authentic relationship happens. This is God's design for community, and it promotes shared purpose, collective worship, love, forgiveness, and human flourishing.

When we choose to live in close proximity to others, seek intimacy in our friendships, and attempt to be vulnerable with our pain, it not only frees us from carrying our burdens alone but it also invites growth. It forces us to live in humility, giving other people the opportunity to accept us despite our flaws—or not. Likewise, when we are given the privilege of seeing similar flaws in those we love and cherish, we, too, receive a life lesson in unconditional love.

This depth of intimacy requires honesty. It leads to accountability, and it is humbling. But it is often in these vulnerable, honest places that we find strength, truth, and growth. Our journey is a shared experience, building on the trials of those who have gone before us and providing scaffolding for the people who will follow. We were never supposed to walk it alone.

Through my pain, God continued to reveal a lack of true intimacy and connection with many of those around me. My busy life had left little time for slow and intimate conversations, shared meals, and awkward vulnerability. Amid changing roles, communities, and locations, I lost many relationships, and it was easy to feel isolated. Withdrawing from activities and community due to my declining health and emotional capacity also meant that I walked through much of this journey feeling very alone.

There is so much to be said for being a part of something, taking action, or serving others as part of a team or church community. It can be complex at times but also fun and invigorating, awakening our hearts to a shared mission and purpose. But if we spend our lives building a team but have no one to call in the middle of the night when we are in distress, grief, or experiencing crippling anxiety—what exactly are we building?

First and foremost, God calls us to friendship and intimacy with Him. When I felt lonely and isolated in my earthly community, God continued to show me the value of connection. We have full access to a God who wants honesty and vulnerability, and He is constantly offering us an invitation to let Him into our lives—even those shadowy places that we would prefer to remain hidden. In John 15:4, Jesus uses the metaphor of a vine and its branches to illustrate the necessity of maintaining intimacy with Him. As a branch bears fruit by remaining in the vine, so we too bear fruit and flourish when we remain attached to the True Vine—Jesus Christ.

God created us in His image—the Holy Trinity of Father, Son, and Spirit—so it is no surprise that we, too, yearn for relationship, intimacy, and connection. Thankfully, there are beautiful and special people whom God has placed around us. People who can handle our shortcomings. People who see the dark parts of us and choose to stay anyway. People with whom we can be ourselves—no façades, no pretending, no show. Yes, sometimes we are hurt by those closest to us. Sometimes, we are betrayed. Sometimes, we let people in and subsequently suffer abuse at their hands. (This can be traumatic and heartbreaking and deserves acknowledgement and care.) But other times, we discover a treasure. To love and be loved by others is the most wonderful blessing, and it is a blessing that deserves our time and energy. So, keep trusting that you will find your tribe. And when you do, hold them close.

I've learned that the people we have around us can make a huge difference in the way we experience the difficulties we are facing. Whether it is simply having a coffee together, enjoying a rom-com and a decent cry, engaging in a robust theological discussion, or offering a compassionate, listening ear—spending time with a trusted friend gives us the time and space to get away from the stresses of life and take a life-giving breath. Sometimes, it looks like having an honest conversation about our mental health or physical struggles. Other times, it's talking about everything *but* church. Or perhaps it's laughing and reminiscing about the old days (if, like me, you're lucky enough to have a few good school friends). Your church is not everything. Jesus is everything. And He is with you wherever you go.

Ministry can be so lonely. When you are in leadership, many people hold you at arm's length. They are polite and loving but not willing to be vulnerable in your presence. Perhaps they don't want to bring you close because of your role or proximity to other leaders. They might not want you to know their business unless it's a crisis they need help with. They may be ashamed of their sin, unaware or unbelieving that you struggle with similar issues! On the other hand, perhaps as a leader, you prefer there to be some distance between you and those you serve. I get it.

That's why it's so important that we find Christian sisters outside of our church. When we insulate ourselves within our small ministry circle, difficult seasons can feel isolating. However, when we foster healthy friendships beyond our immediate context, we create a wider safety net to catch us if we become untethered in our ministry journey. We develop a tribe of safe and spiritually healthy people with whom we can speak freely, cry, or pray, knowing they will not feel threatened by our doubts, questions, and fears. Many times, a rational and deliberate conversation with a wise person outside of our ministry context is necessary for us to receive the truth or correction we need in a given situation or season.

As I began to navigate new relationships in light of all God had shown me through this process of change, I finally felt the freedom to bring my whole self to the table and be open and honest about my challenges, strengths, and weaknesses. I had a new confidence to be content with who I was and what I had walked through. I was able to stand on my convictions and the issues I was passionate about. I was able to have hard conversations. And I could finally accept it was okay for people to say no to me or decide that I wasn't the right person for them. Amid the honesty, laughter, and mess, I began to create new connections. Deep and honest connections without a platform or façade. This required knowing myself well. Through the counselling and heart work I had done, I had not only come to know my vulnerabilities, my weaknesses, my personality and my thought processes, but I had the freedom to openly express them. This was new for me. Instead of entering into new relationships with a veneer of strength and perfection, I chose humility, knowing that whether or not I was accepted by others, I was accepted by God who wired me this way. I'm a sucker for personality tests, especially ones that help me understand the way I think, what I need from others, and how other people interact with me. I know they are not everyone's cup of tea, but over the years, some have helped me to better understand myself and build relationships with others.

Finding your tribe is not just about embarking on new relationships. I am so grateful for the few friends who stayed with me through this whole journey—you are pure gold. I am so thankful for those of you who sat with my snotty, red face as I cried over FaceTime, who prayed for me over the phone and in the quiet places I never knew about, and who had the courage to be honest and speak loving truth into my life. Thank you! That you would see all of me and still choose to be here with me is such a gift. I am also so grateful for some of the new friendships that have been forged that feel like spring rain. You are choosing to connect with the imperfect me, and I am here for it!

God will bring people into your life who are ready for all of you at just the right time. He might bring further wholeness to your mind before He introduces you to these people. Conversely, He may bring people in the midst of your mess who will offer to help pull you out of the pit you have fallen into. Open your eyes, friend. When I opened mine, I found new relationships—people who were willing to support and carry me through a difficult season and be there to cheer me on when the sun came out again. I found strength in long-distance, longstanding relationships—those who let me ugly cry and encouraged me when I wanted to give up. But another beautiful discovery has been in reconnecting with some of our church family again after a period of healing and processing. The circumstances may be different, but the connection is the same. I say this to remind you that intentional, authentic, honest relationships do make an impact. Even after a long time apart, people can still hold a special place for you and appreciate your vulnerability, your sacrifice. So, make room for these church connections in your life because they matter—more than you know.

Friend, please don't get so busy building, reaching and growing in ministry that there is no space for close, intimate and honest relationships. Find your tribe. They may be few, but they will be the net that catches you, challenges you, and encourages you. They will see it all and love you anyway, pulling you in even closer when you feel like you're falling over the edge. So, make room for them. Slow down for them. And always be your authentic self. There's no room for façade in tribal living.

# Treasure Connection

There is so much delight to be found in the conversations and connections we have outside of church ministry. Our neighbours, work colleagues, old school friends and fellow school mums are all treasures worth investing in. We are the salt and light in their world. Whether they are open to Jesus or seem to be a closed door, we are called to love them and share our joy with them.

I remember living next to a beautiful Muslim woman when we purchased our first home. Our babies were the same age, and we were both stay-at-home mums during that season. Our different worldviews did not matter when we laughed and commiserated about sleepless nights or toilet-training episodes over cups of tea. We had a natural affinity because of our shared experiences, and I always hoped she felt welcomed by her Christian neighbour next door. Later, when our new Korean neighbours moved in, we took over some baking. They returned the generosity by cooking us a Korean BBQ—it was a win-win! When we broke into their house to save it from a fire that was smoking and about to ignite their kitchen, they bought us cake and watermelon to say thank you.

Friend, the people outside of your ministry matter. They matter to Jesus, and they should matter to us. Treasure them, find out their names, practice hospitality, and be generous. Share your kindness with the drive-thru barista or pay it forward to the person behind you. Tell that mum with the toddler in meltdown that she is doing a great job. Stop to offer that person carrying heavy groceries a ride home. Tell that woman that you love her shoes (my kids are constantly embarrassed by me when I do these things!). It's funny how a small act of kindness can spark a connection or make a real difference. Find and keep friends and connections outside of the walls of your church and ministry—not with an agenda to bring them to a service but to love them right where they are.

I regret not investing as much time into external relationships as I could have. Since there was so much to do and so many people to reach, I focused much of my time and energy on my immediate ministry circle and bringing new people into the church building. Our whole world revolved around our ministry schedule. I declined school mum outings, kids' playdates, family sports commitments, and evening classes. I neglected people to whom I could have been a powerful witness. I spent so much time with my Christian family that I forgot others might benefit from my connection and company who needed the message of Jesus, too.

As our family healed, we began to look outwards and see the treasure that lay around us. My husband decided to coach our son's soccer team (though he had no idea about soccer himself), and we were suddenly thrown together with a group of people we'd only just met. None of them were Christian or moved in any of our ministry circles, but the fun and friendship we formed over that season was a breath of fresh air. The integrity and dedication my husband brought to the game and the way he loved on those boys was a shining light. We made time for each other, and the connections we made still stand. What treasure there is to behold outside the walls of our church buildings!

I heard a message from a visiting preacher recently, Shane Willard, who said that "Christianity is a life to demonstrate, not an argument to win." Every time we interact with our neighbours, our kids' teachers, our hairdresser, our physiotherapist, etc., we have an opportunity to be a city on a hill. So, treasure every person. Listen to the Holy Spirit's prompts about generosity and hospitality—they are there, believe me! Go beyond the discomfort and fear of opening up and choose to be an encourager, a giver.

Perhaps you experience anxiety at the thought of speaking to someone you don't know. Maybe you are in the midst of a struggle, and your emotional capacity does not venture beyond your own home. This is where you are right now, and it's okay. But I pray that one day, as the healing work of God permeates your heart, you will also be an encouraging voice for others. I pray that as they face life's difficulties, you will uplift them and offer them the very hope you are praying for right now in your own life.

Friend, we need people. God created other imperfect humans so that we might all come together in this messy humanity and love each other dearly. Look up and look out. There is opportunity all around you. Love your neighbours. Shine your light brightly. People want to know what

Jesus would do, how He would respond to them, and how He might love them. Let's show them that!

# Weakness as a Gift

As Christians, we believe there is strength in our weakness because of God's grace and His power that is evident despite our humanity (2 Corinthians 12:10). Although this scripture points to the weakness and fragility of our human nature, we tend to focus more on the promise of strength. And while we *should* cling to God's promises amid seasons of hardship, persecution, and difficulty, we cannot have one without the other. If we are to receive His strength and power, we also need to accept the reality of our weakness. Showing humility in response to our misgivings, sins, doubts, emotional distress, fears, addictions or difficulties gives wings to His power, which is made perfect through our weaknesses, faults, and inadequacies. I had completely missed this. The Collins Dictionary defines weakness as a 'lack of strength' or 'an inadequate or defective quality, as in a person's character; slight fault or defect'. So, even in my lack, faults, and defects, God's power and strength have the opportunity to shine through me. It's interesting because, in my attempt to be strong in all areas, my pride had become my much-needed undoing. Choosing to embrace my weaknesses was both humbling and freeing.

Some things surfaced in my journey that I had long suppressed as weaknesses. I am a feeler. Some might call me an empath. My psychologist says my mirror neurons are firing. This means I strongly feel empathy and compassion for others. My emotions sometimes overflow from my eyes and stream down my face—well, probably more than sometimes. I am passionate about justice and everything Jesus said about looking after the poor, the widow, and the rejected. I see it, and I feel it. This can be to my detriment, but it is also a gift that allows me to do the work I do and write my heart on paper.

Ever since I was a child, my emotions would quickly surface every time I was challenged by someone. Whether it was a work meeting, a pastoral discussion or an honest marriage check-in, the tears would flow—whether I liked it or not. Somewhere deep within me was this sense that if I wasn't doing everything right, I was incompetent. I am a rule follower and have always hated getting in trouble. So, this drive to do it all and do it perfectly was born from a deep insecurity about how I was perceived by others and a need to feel or look competent and able.

Fancy that! It doesn't quite fit in with what the Bible says about weakness, does it? Christ's strength is made perfect in our weakness. To experience His strength and power, then, we need to humble ourselves and accept our weaknesses. What a load off that is! I don't have to do what she's doing. I don't have to strive to be a leader like him. I don't have to prove that I can do it all as a wife and mother. It doesn't have to be right or perfect all the time. I *can* make mistakes.

Oh, God's upside-down kingdom really does mess with our human thinking! How freeing it was to understand that humbling myself— accepting my weaknesses and letting go of my pride—offered an opportunity to enjoy and experience God's strength and power. Without this humility, I may not even know the true extent of it because God shows up in the biggest ways when I accept the weakness of my humanity.

It is easy to train ourselves to find the faults and fix them. Review the problem and find the solution so that it never happens again. Perfect the image, and create something that will bring people in. We try to curate the 'perfect' atmosphere so that God will move, and people will be touched by Him. We understand that the world is obsessed with image, so we try to compete for people's attention—by creating something exactly the same. We cannot comprehend that God still moves despite our imperfections, our imperfect buildings, our imperfect bodies, and our myriad of mistakes. He doesn't need us to give Him a room or a run sheet or a smooth link between songs. In Exodus 20:25, the Israelites are given clear instructions by God (through Moses) about how to build an altar in the desert wilderness. Instead of asking them to polish, cut and create perfect, identical stones, He told them to use natural, uncut ones. The Israelites were on the move, and God required their hearts, their obedience, and humility. Asking the Israelites to use simple, imperfect stones to erect a place of worship to Him shows us that God doesn't require our perfection, our works, or our striving. He's simply after our hearts.

I had always hated the way my emotions spilled over, and it would frustrate me when the tears flowed, and I felt I had no control. It wasn't until I came to God in broken pieces that He was able to reveal the beauty in who He had created me to be. It wasn't until I acknowledged Him in my weakness that He lovingly pointed out the things that I needed to surrender to Him and those I needed Him to heal and change. Now that I have a better understanding of why I respond the way I do, I can harness the goodness in it. While working through some of the beliefs and motivations underlying my insecurity and competence, I have been able to understand this inherent part of me that was placed there by God. The part of me that feels deeply for others and grieves at the sight of injustice and suffering. The part of me that listens willingly and compassionately to other people's stories with a desire for greater understanding. The part of me—that for so long felt like a thorn in my side— that is actually a gift placed inside of me so that I may accomplish God's purposes in my life.

God is asking for our imperfections, and He delights in what we bring Him. Although our offering is limited, God wants it. He's willing to accept it. Struggling, hurting, broken—He wants it all. He is not impressed by how much we do for Him or how smooth and shiny our lives are. Rather, He is interested in our obedience, humility, and love. So, let's build Him an altar with all our imperfect pieces and acknowledge His power in all the weak and unedited areas of our hearts.

# Something Has to Break

After much reflection and soul-searching, I finally grasped what God had been trying to tell me during this barren winter season. I had been hurtling through a vortex of physical, spiritual and emotional pain as my fear and frustration mounted. Bitterness had begun to take hold in my heart, and I was wrestling with unforgiveness towards myself and others. The arrival of winter, however, forced me to stop everything I was doing and gain a deeper perspective and understanding of my situation. Something had to break. Something had to change.

God had given me free will to make my own decisions, and now I had to choose to stop holding onto things that I knew were hindering my purpose and obedience to Christ, creating unhealthy patterns or relationships. Whilst life-altering decision-making can seem unwise or even irrational during dark and difficult seasons, for others, the journey into the depths can provide transformational spiritual clarity and insight. In some cases, a deep shift is necessary to interrupt the trajectory of our lives and act as a catalyst for something new, different, and needed. I had to turn my heart away from other people's expectations and applause and turn towards my Creator. I had to break the hold of perfection and performance and choose to embrace the mess. I had to enforce boundaries while I explored my faith, healed from pain, and established healthier habits. I had to break away from unhealthy relationships and connections that were prompting Holy Spirit checks on my spirit. I had to say no to the wrong things and pick up the things that were right for me.

Winter was my interruption. It was the interlude I needed to reflect on the state of my heart and the difficult journey that had brought me to this crossroads. I knew I couldn't continue the way I had been living, and it was time for me to embark on a different path. As the desolation of winter began to ease, the promise of spring whispered in my ear. The barrenness had created a clean slate for something new.

# Winter Reflection

Consider if there is grief in some area of your life that you have not allowed yourself to express fully.

🥀 What misguided beliefs may have stifled the gift of lament?

_____

_____

_____

_____

_____

_____

_____

_____

_____

_____

_____

🥀 Where might God be encouraging you to develop deep and authentic connections with others?

_____

_____

_____

_____

_____

_____

_____

_____

_____

_____

_____

_____

How could you create greater accountability with your most trusted relationships?

_____

_____

_____

_____

_____

_____

_____

_____

_____

_____

What area of weakness is God asking you to acknowledge and surrender to Him?

_____

_____

_____

_____

_____

_____

_____

_____

_____

_____

_____

🌹 What things need to break in your life?

_____

_____

_____

_____

_____

_____

_____

_____

_____

_____

_____

_____

PART THREE

# SPRING

*Spring speaks of newness, of fresh growth. The cold earth gives way, nature peeling back as things formed underneath break through. There is a sudden sense of hope and expectation as the new is birthed, youth and vitality making their way through. Breath is captured once again and creativity is exhaled into the atmosphere, colour and brightness intertwined with the wisdom which was gained through the dark of the night.*

# Spring: Grow

It was slow at first
The season of change
The subtle colours, ideas, thoughts
The questions and doubts
The unanswered
The avoided conversations

Suddenly the roots of change
Burst open into this soil I was tending
No longer able to stay hidden

And here it began
This force, unstoppable
I could not keep it buried anymore

# Into the Wrestle

It wasn't until my body began to heal physically that I realised God was doing an even deeper work within me—something I had been unable to address fully until my healing journey began. This process took me back to my childhood, unravelling layers of belief and understanding relating to both God and myself. Let me tell you, it hurt. I was forced to confront who I had become and the life I had created around me, characterised by lost dreams, relationships, and opportunities. I had to accept that I had allowed idols to take root in my life, my mind, and my family, and I was faced with the disappointing realisation of how they had impacted those closest to me, especially my husband and children.

It was a confusing time. As I transformed more into the woman I believed God designed me to be, I knew I needed to address anything in my life that was unhealthy or unhelpful. Like threshing the wheat, I exposed and separated the things that were necessary and valuable for my growth and left the rest behind. As I journeyed through this season, I wrote and wrestled. And through the hardest of times, God has shown me the most beautiful of things. He has opened my eyes and revealed His love, His forgiveness, and His wisdom. Some of these treasures are just between me and God. But, dear sister, others are for sharing with you.

# Do That Thing

I have always had a heart to serve God, serve others, and serve God's house. I found my purpose in doing whatever needed to be done. I filled any gap that needed to be filled and served on any team where there was space. I led where I was asked to lead and put my heart and energy into whatever I did. My intentions were always good—as were the hearts of those who led and served alongside me. I served joyfully (most of the time!), and God moved powerfully as lives were transformed before my eyes. As I witnessed people coming to know Christ and the light of Christ shining through them into their own families and communities, I felt like I had found the winning ticket. But had I?

Scripture uses the analogy of a body to highlight the importance of unity and diversity within the church. 1 Corinthians 12:12-30 tells us that we each have a different role and function in Christ's body but are equally valued and should show equal concern for each part. Created with a specific purpose, we were not designed to be like someone else or chase after their giftings. Rather, we are called to steward *our* God-given calling so that, together, we are united in God's Kingdom purpose.

Notice that Scripture doesn't say, "Be the hand and nose and liver." It doesn't say, "Become skilled in every part and role." It doesn't promise that God will give you the capacity to outwork every role within the church. In the Parable of the Talents in Matthew 25:14-30, we are told that God places something in each of our hands, and it is up to us how we grow and harvest that which He has given us. So, if we are only one part of the body and God has only placed specific things in our hands, why do we feel the need to do it all and outwork every different part? What/whom are we trying to appease? While we have good intentions, I believe this mindset to fill every gap and go wherever we are asked to by others can get in the way of the specific places and people God has called us to. We must regularly ask ourselves: *Where is God's will and wisdom in my decision-making? What has He called me to do in this season, and for what purpose has He given me grace?*

I know God has called me to specific things that make my heart full. I also know what I am good at. I find, however, that my strengths and my passions can sometimes struggle to synchronise. In a ministry environment, it is very easy for us to do the things we are good at and neglect the activities that bring us joy. It is also easy to get caught up in what *needs* to be done rather than what God has called us to do. When we are constantly reacting out of urgency or necessity instead of first seeking our purpose, we risk becoming spiritually dehydrated. Whilst we might still be doing great and valuable work, the passions and pursuits God has created us to do are not being fulfilled. We are spending our time being an ear when He has called us to be an eye.

Why would God grace us with skills that we are not so passionate about? Why, for example, would He create an incredible administrative gift in someone whose heart is geared towards discipleship? Why might someone who is passionate about building connection and relationship, be gifted in building systems and processes? God makes no mistakes. He does these things on purpose and for a purpose. So what happens if we surrender both our skills and passions to God, trusting that He will bring them together to form whatever wonderful masterpiece He has planned for us at just the right time? I am reminded of Queen Esther in the book of Esther—a very beautiful woman who captured the eyes of the king. Although God graced her with incredible beauty that catapulted her to places where others could not go, her fulfilment did not stem from her outward appearance. What gave her true meaning and purpose was her relationship with God and her passion for her people. Ultimately, God would create a beautiful mosaic with her story—a coming together of her God-given gifts, a passionate heart for God, and a mission to save her people. One would not have happened without the other.

In First and Second Samuel, we read about the life of King David, who started his journey as a shepherd boy. Whilst the skills he learned during this time—fighting off wild animals to save his sheep and becoming competent in playing an instrument—helped to prepare him for his future, becoming a skilled shepherd boy was not his ultimate purpose. His abilities served a much bigger plan. If David had simply continued to look after his sheep and play his harp to his family and animals, he would have missed out on the future God had for him. David's first passion was God, who prepared and propelled him into his calling and future as a king. But without one, there would not be the other. It is often both/and, although the coming together of these things is a journey of discovery in itself.

Sometimes we are obliged to use our skills out of financial necessity rather than having a passion for the role. I certainly did because it seemed necessary, and I realise that so many of us feel backed against the wall in this area. I remember a time when I left full-time church ministry for a great administrative role in order to keep our heads above water. It was a fantastic team with strong leadership, but though I was graced with the skills for the role, it didn't inspire joy and passion within me. When I was speaking to a ministry counsellor before starting the role, he told me the job was not suited to my temperament and unique calling, and I should put a time limit on it—no more than six months. Did I listen? No. I let our family's financial situation dictate my choices, and since I loved my team and was comfortable in that environment, I stayed far longer than I had anticipated. While maintaining my administrative position, I also continued to volunteer in ministry roles that I didn't feel purposed to do. Desiring to serve and respond to the needs around me, I didn't speak up and have meaningful conversations about what I was being asked to do. Ultimately, my lack of trust in God to fulfil our family's needs or provide me with a purposeful role led me down a slippery slope. Despite being graced with the skills to do these jobs well, neither my professional role nor my ministry roles brought true fulfilment, passion, or joy.

I do not mean to sound ungrateful. God was incredibly kind to us during these years, providing for our family, often through the generosity of others, enabling my husband to continue in his ministry role. I also need to take responsibility for the choices I made in this season. I chose to say yes; I chose to stay; I let the fear of honest and difficult conversations get in the way of speaking up at all. I chose to continue with things that I knew were not bringing fulfilment. I also realise that my perspectives come from a place of privilege. To have access to choice, an education, and the freedom to move from one opportunity to another is a privilege many will not know. But how are we being good stewards of our privilege? What amazing things might God be calling us to when we have the means to choose our next steps?

Ultimately, we are each responsible for stewarding the call and purpose that God has placed within us, and His timing is always perfect. During this period of pain and confusion, I made a bold move—a job change. I knew I could not remain stuck in this place of heaviness and hopelessness, and part of the solution required me to understand and be obedient to the calling and giftings God had given me. I had reached a tipping point and begun to understand the relationship between our God-given calling and how we choose to spend our time, energy, and resources. I did not know exactly what I was called to do, but I knew my future needed to include work that fulfilled me. Identifying the attributes I valued—compassion, grace, justice, integrity, and love in action—was my starting point. I had allowed them to be stifled for so long, but now they dictated the direction I needed to go in my vocational future. I came to understand that working on staff in a church or being in church ministry full time was not the pinnacle of our Christian calling and not something we all need to aspire to. In understanding the part we all have to play, God helped me to see that every Christian is involved in ministry somewhere, whether it be at the local playgroup as a stay-at-home parent, as a high-level executive, as a volunteer or missionary, and in every field. God requires us to step out and be the person He designed us to be, wherever that leads us. It is not always seen or heard by those around us, but how we humbly serve and steward the calling God has on our life is seen by God.

I prayed for the right job, and God provided over and above what I could have imagined for myself. It was an answer to my prayers. This role allowed me to draw on my Social Work experience to come alongside children and families, supporting children in the school environment to grow, develop and flourish in their actions towards others, their perspective of the world around them, and their internal processes. The role allowed me to outwork my relational gifts whilst making room for creativity and encompassing my administrative skills and systematic thinking. And when pain thrashed me in the first few months, I held on so tight, feeling secure in my trust that I was in the right place. When I felt like quitting or breaking down due to the pain, I held on moment by moment. Through my healing, God began to release such joy in me for the work I was doing. I had a newfound purpose, gratitude, and hope for the plans God had for my future. And I was so grateful to God that nothing is ever wasted. No pain, no change, no process. Stepping into this new position helped me to understand why my previous role had been necessary. It was a natural stepping stone, and without it, I may not have discovered this exciting new door I was now walking through.

It wasn't long before God began to reveal how my administrative gifting and my ability to plan and apply processes were valuable skills in this role and could be utilised to enhance my workplace. My eye for detail and passion for words created a pathway for new resources and group communications. Whilst being obedient to the call of God in my life, He allowed me to see how my skills and experiences complemented my God-given purpose. I finally understood that the passions He had placed within me were there to guide me so that I might journey with Him and be fulfilled.

A burden that has been heavy to carry at times is my passion for social justice and my determination to create a better world for those in need. I am particularly drawn to the areas of human trafficking, sex slavery, and poverty. In 2019, I was privileged to go to Cambodia with an organisation that rescues and rehabilitates young girls who have been impacted by the sex trafficking trade. Cambodia opened my eyes, and from the moment I stepped out of the airport, I felt alive, knowing God had ripped open my heart for this place and its people. One of the positive markers that directed me to my new vocational role was the organisation's heart for mission work, especially in Cambodia. Our shared passion in this area was what got me across the line and confirmed in my heart that it was the right position for me.

In 2023, I was able to travel back to Cambodia with a team from my workplace to work with communities in immense poverty. We visited numerous organisations involved in the rescue and rehabilitation of young women and children from human trafficking, and I was even able to train a school team there concerning the line of work I am involved with. These two trips have been some of the greatest joys of my life. God has a way of working it all together for our good—Romans 8:28 confirms this!

God has placed passions and callings within us for a reason, and this is not something we can simply ignore within the church environment. In any context, there will be times when we need to knuckle down and do whatever needs to get done. Maybe it's during the initial stages of starting a church when it's all hands on deck or during a time of transition when church members require extra communication, pastoral care, and guidance. Perhaps it is required when you are starting a business or working towards a specific goal. We can't be naïve enough to think that everything we do is going to be sunshine and roses. But these times of exertion should be seasonal. Let's keep in mind that our skills and experience complement the larger purpose God has designed for us as we work together as part of His body. And just to be clear, I am talking about purpose here, not pleasure. The Bible is very clear about chasing pleasures and the strife this causes us. Remember, God's purpose is pure, values others, and exists to bring Him the glory, not ourselves.

Friend, perhaps it's time for you to do an audit and reflect on all the things you give your time, space and heart to. Talk to God about the activities that fill your cup and bring joy and purpose to your life, and be mindful of those that deplete or exhaust you. Take note of anything that detracts you from your specific God-given purpose and recognise the skills that complement your passions. Ask yourself if you are constantly reacting to the needs all around you, or are you listening to God and doing what *He* has called you to do? Needs will always exist, and there is always more to be done—Matthew 9:35-38 tells us that the harvest is ripe and there is a need for workers. Yet, we need to exert wisdom in the way we respond to these needs or our 'yes' attitude could be our undoing. It is not selfish to focus on the activities we feel particularly called to or to put boundaries on our time and areas of serving. Rather, it shows wisdom and maturity in our relationship with Christ to confidently trust the passions He has placed within us. When we stay in our lane and allow others to flourish in theirs, there is unity in the body as we all work together as one. So, say yes to the things that complement your calling and allow God's purpose to guide your ministry journey.

How gracious of God to bring me back from the brink into a spacious and fulfilling place! I hope this encourages you that God's love for us is exuberant and overflowing, and when we abide in Him, He expands our hearts so that we can be exuberant and overflowing also. When we are living in His grace, we can trust that He will work through us so that our fruitful lives can serve as a reflection of His grace, His power, and His faithfulness.

# Physical Limits

As God continued to heal my body, I became more attuned to my heart rate, the tension in my shoulders, my sleeping patterns, and the stressors that threatened to trigger my pain. I had come to understand that my physical healing was only the first part of the puzzle, and there were many more things God needed to address spiritually and emotionally. My physical body was the part of me that finally broke down and said, "Enough!" But it was also the first to pick itself back up again and partner with me on the journey of healing.

I think we often view our bodies as being distinct from our relationship with God. They are just a conduit, a thing that is neither here nor there. And because we do not value our bodies as the very instruments we need to outwork God's purposes in our lives, we do not treat them with the wisdom and respect they deserve. We do not fully grasp the impact that our minds and spirits have on our bodies and the way they are interwoven, working hand in hand. We treat one but not the other when, in fact, every part of us comes together to make a whole.

Psalm 139:14 tells us we are fearfully and wonderfully made, our bodies and our innermost being created by and lovingly handled by God. We underestimate the love and care and intricate detail God designed our bodies to hold and communicate. And too often, we choose to ignore the subtle or glaringly obvious messages our bodies are sending us.

Matthew 11:28-30 in *The Message* perfectly summed up how I was feeling during this season and offers hope in a God who understands our physical needs:

> *Are you tired? Worn out? Burned out on religion?*
> *Come to me. Get away with me and you'll recover*
> *your life. I'll show you how to take a real rest. Walk*
> *with me and work with me—watch how I do it. Learn*
> *the unforced rhythms of grace. I won't lay anything*
> *heavy or ill-fitting on you. Keep company with me*
> *and you'll learn to live freely and lightly.*

Reading this scripture called for me to take a breath, sigh, and allow my shoulders to relax and trust in the One who was holding me and could handle the fullness of everything I was going through. I was doing far more than I had been instructed by God to do—too much striving and proving and reacting and perfecting. The myriad of church meetings, work and family commitments and financial pressure did not create a recipe that was conducive to peace, rest, joy, and purpose. But I kept going and going and going, ordering my body to move into alignment with my mission and lifestyle. I chose not to heed its warnings, and in the end, my body rebelled against me.

I love the story of Elijah in 1 Kings 19. This incredible man of God had come to the end of himself and was facing a literal desert moment. Yet, this spiritually significant experience was also a very practical one. Helpless, exhausted, and physically unable to go on, Elijah lay down under a tree and had a nap. An angel woke him up and gave him something to eat and drink before he went back to sleep again. Then, the angel woke him again, giving him even more food and water before he set out onto the next stage of his journey. This story contains many more lessons and insights, but what I have come to realise here is that God cares about our physical needs. When we are exhausted, He knows just what we need and can provide for us. God didn't simply show up in all His power and glory (though He could have), give Elijah a shot of adrenalin, and tell him to keep going. God didn't order Elijah to get up because he had important godly work to do. He was not scolded, mocked, or questioned. Instead, in His compassion and grace, God gave Elijah exactly what he needed at that moment: physical rest and sustenance. We, too, need to listen and pay attention to what our body is trying to communicate. God is not afraid of our humanity. He is not angry if we feel tired and need to rest. He designed us to live in bodies that have limitations—and we all have them, no matter our capabilities. At times, He may call us to break through our physical limitations and rely on Him for the impossible. But He will let us know. We can trust Him and His wisdom—if we choose to listen.

For a long time, I did not listen. As a night owl and someone who generally thinks better late at night (it's 10 p.m. as I write this), I found it easy to work late at night—meeting deadlines, approving media pieces or designs, or working on rosters. However, I never adjusted the rest of my schedule, maintaining an unhealthy rhythm of early work wakeups, night meetings, and school arrangements. I was pushing through my limitations and giving out far more than I could replenish. And after ignoring other indicators in my life for so long, my body decided it had had enough.

Remaining in a long season of healing forced me to listen and be intentional. Whilst my health was improving, it was still teetering on the edge, and I knew I needed to guard the temple of my body during this process of transformation. This meant understanding my limitations—physically, mentally, and emotionally—listening to wise instructions from professionals about what my body was lacking, and choosing to value my body for the soul God had placed within it. I began to take note of the things that reduced my anxiety and stress like early morning walks before work, deep breathing, and healthy food intake. I realised that walking in nature, especially near the water or through the bush, releases joy in my soul and gives me perspective. It also allows me to take deeper breaths, which encourages greater levels of oxytocin and helps me to feel good. I also trained myself to go to bed earlier after recognising that if I go to bed after 10 p.m., my body gets a second wind, which can keep me up until the wee hours. When I go to bed later than 10 p.m., I am making a conscious decision to stay awake much later and no matter how many times I try to rationalise it to myself, I almost always regret it. I realised that although I get energy and joy from being social and around people, I also need to refuel in quiet and calm spaces alone. This was news to me as I had always considered myself a raging extrovert. But recognising the personal benefits when I leave margin for quiet contemplation has allowed me to become comfortable with stillness and solitude and learn to say no. This season was slow and steady, and it did not come easily to me. Yet, despite regular pain, mixed feelings, and anxious residue, I did finally start to sense a change.

My physical body may have begun the healing process, but there was still so much to uncover, work through, and change. Spring brought new growth, but it was a painful process. Growth meant acknowledging hard truths—about myself and others. Growth meant tuning my ear and being obedient to the Holy Spirit, even when it felt uncomfortable. Growth meant highlighting my sins, making changes within my relationships, altering habits, and taking slow steps forward and many steps back. Even during seasons of improvement, we can sometimes get derailed. We think that once the worst of winter has thawed, we can do all and be all that we once were. We run the risk of reliving the same experiences over and over again. We learn how to cope with the cycles of pain and brokenness, but God does not call us to simply cope. He wants so much more than that for us than burnout, heal, repeat. Our bodies need so much more than that. God wants the deep, the underlying, and the ugly. He wants our histories, our experiences, and the shameful, dark intentions of our messy, broken hearts. It's up to us to choose what we bring to Him in our spring seasons—how far we want to go and how much we are willing to give Him. Spring became a time of unmasking and deep learning.

Now when I choose to say no, guilt no longer plagues me. Accepting my limitations is a new place for me to reside. Having enough humility to say that I cannot get to something, don't have the capacity for something or know that someone else can do it instead is a work in progress. I am still learning! I remember my counsellor reassuring me once that if I took a step back, the world would still turn. The church service would still take place. Someone would fulfil the role—and even if they didn't, it was not my burden to carry. God knew we had limitations when He made us, and if He's okay with them, why aren't we? Whether it's our perfectionism and pride, a need to prove our work ethic, or the pressure we feel from ourselves or others, many things can lead us to ignore what our bodies are trying to tell us. And if we don't listen, our neglect will eventually catch up with us.

I am not saying God never gives us the grace and instruction to defy the odds and push through our limitations. Many people can rise to great heights and achieve incredible feats with their bodies. We each have a unique calling from God, and our bodies are all different. But one thing we do have in common is that our bodies are not superhuman entities. We are fallible. God will give us the strength and capacity to do the things He has purposed for us to do. But that is all we need to do.

If we want our bodies to experience real change, we need to get off the hamster wheel and listen and be obedient to the promptings of the Holy Spirit. So, listen to your body. Listen to the tiredness, the pain, the lack of sleep. Listen to the whisper in your spirit when God is telling you to stop, keep going, or try something new. Your body is a temple of the Holy Spirit, and it's time to find a rhythm of grace which encourages physical flourishing, good health, helpful habits, and a spirit that sings with the evidence of God's joy and intimacy.

# Purpose in the Pain

I remember how I felt when I entered my dark winter season: the emotions that surprised and disappointed me, the loss of control, and my lack of connection and capacity. I'm not proud of some of the things I said or did in this season. I had trained as a social worker, dedicated time to justice causes, and believed wholeheartedly in the redemptive, healing grace offered by Jesus Christ. And yet, as a younger, more inexperienced woman, I typically shied away from people whose lives I deemed too difficult, too complex, too dramatic. I was well educated, raised in a stable, Christian home, and experienced in matters of health and wellbeing; yet, I harboured frustration towards those who were unable to fix issues in their own lives. Part of me felt ill-equipped and helpless to understand their trauma and mental health challenges, not realising that they simply needed a kind word and a listening ear rather than a one-word solution from me. I thought I was invincible, and my privilege provided the perfect backdrop for my arrogance and ignorance. I had no real understanding of other people's pain and trauma happening around me, and I lacked compassion and empathy for their unique and complex situations.

I remember the shame of wondering how I—a social worker and a Christian no less—could have ended up here! My shame initially stopped me from being vulnerable and honest with the people who loved me most. I was so independent, stubborn, and self-reliant that I struggled to come to terms with the fact that my mind and body were not fully under my control.

God was asking me to eat a big piece of humble pie.

And whilst humbling, the pain I experienced allowed my empathy and compassion towards others to extend further than it had before. Once the fog started to lift and I began to share my journey with others, I discovered a new perspective. I was given new eyes to see others, empathise with their trauma and brokenness, and share in their grief. The Holy Spirit filled up my heart with a deeper love for those around me, helping me to identify with their suffering—chronic pain, broken thoughts, doubt, fear, and emptiness—in ways that enabled me to love them more. Alongside this newfound understanding, I discovered a greater purpose.

Wisdom is for sharing. The lessons learned on our journeys bring wisdom into our lives. Even if it is hard-earned, revealing painful truths about ourselves or others, it is wisdom all the same. If God is working all things together for good, perhaps greater wisdom, understanding and empathy is the 'good' that can spring from these dark seasons. We become a community of people who understand the human condition and, when able, are willing to support others through similar experiences, pointing them towards Jesus and the wholeness and healing only He can provide. If we make a choice (it's still a choice) to let God do His gentle work within us—relinquishing our fear, our cynicism, our unforgiveness, and our pride—we allow Him to use our pain and make something beautiful out of the ashes of our lives. It requires total surrender of our hardened hearts, but oh! The joy that comes from knowing that our pain serves a greater purpose!

Friend, you may not feel it right now or see an end in sight. But God has a funny way of turning everything around for good (Romans 8:28). At some point in the future, once the sting has lessened and the healing of your heart resembles scars rather than open wounds, your pain will transform into something beautiful. Trust me when I tell you that the depth of your understanding and the vulnerability, wisdom and compassion you show towards others will be a bright spark of hope to those who need it most. Our pain is never wasted. Rather, it serves a greater purpose, enabling us to relate to the suffering of others in a way that is uniquely personal and valuable.

I continued to be a work in progress (I still am!) as God uncovered layers of disordered thinking and selfish ambition and shed light on the stressors to which I was most vulnerable. As I grew in understanding and my emotional capacity increased, God highlighted patterns of behaviour and thinking within me that needed to change and baggage that I continued to carry. Some of these patterns were learned or taught. Some were intergenerational. Some were borne from survival—residue from the dark nights I had struggled through.

Though I was in a season of increased energy and health, I could not move on in full whilst these patterns of control, distrust, frustration and fear persisted. Thankfully, with the help of incredible Christian counsellors, psychologists, and friends, I was able to acknowledge these patterns and accept they were unhealthy. Slowly and gently, God touched, highlighted and asked me to surrender one burden at a time. I believe He allowed me to walk through these autumn, winter and spring seasons so that in summer, He could give me the strength to let go completely.

I can tell you that this journey of discovery does not stop. There is no endpoint. I was discussing with a friend recently that as we get older, the journey changes and grows, but it is still a journey. Until we pass on from this earth, God will keep working in us, and each new adventure reveals new potential for learning and opportunities to understand Him more. There are always new areas of our lives we can surrender and different facets of His personality to explore.

As I regained my confidence, it was not a false confidence in people, accolades, possessions, or a controlled environment. Rather, it was rooted in God. I let go of the people-pleasing, keeping up appearances, and trying to fit the mould. I cared less about the opinions of others and more about what God thought of me. My shame was gone. My pain and brokenness led me to a place of full acceptance of my God-given identity. My subsequent healing created a pathway towards a better understanding of who I was and who He had designed me to be. I also got a renewed perspective of God's design for family.

I know when I talk about family, I talk about the deepest part of us. The deepest love and the deepest scars. The deepest hope and the deepest woe. The deepest joys and the deepest regrets. I am sorry if just the mention of family brings pain you cannot bear or triggers memories you don't want to remember. I pray God is holding your hand as you walk and work through your particular journey. For the purposes of this book, I want to talk about families in the context of church ministry. Our families see the absolute best and worst of us, and as parents, leaders, or servants in the house of God, our families are sometimes neglected, or worse, become collateral damage instead of being central to our mission and ministry.

God has a unique plan for each of us, but He also has a purpose for our families. God created us to be in unity with one another. Our children's lives and thoughts matter to Him. Our spouse's hopes and dreams matter. The people closest to us who feel like family—their voices matter, too. Yet somewhere along the way, as I pursued 'all the things' and pushed ahead, I neglected the unity of my family.

I used to idolise a very well-known Christian speaker, and I was completely in awe of the things God was doing through her to initiate incredible change. I remember seeing social media posts about her travelling with her children on ministry trips, wheeling them in their prams through airports, staying in hotels, and visiting new places. When someone once said to me that I could be like her one day, I was honoured. So, I went to work being all about the ministry. My husband and I served alongside one another, involving our children in every moment or trying to find babysitters where possible. We had no family nearby so our children didn't have grandparents and cousins to be with, learn from, and enjoy. It was just us. Our church family was our family, and we made it work. But I don't think God calls us to 'make it work'. I think He calls us to thrive, to flourish in every season like a tree planted by a stream (Psalm 1:3).

I was so inspired by this famous figure that I thought I needed to drag my kids everywhere, meet those late-night deadlines, and make the most of every opportunity to lead, pastor others, serve, and keep the mission moving forward. We said no to our kids joining sports teams due to all the games and practices we could not commit to. We said no to rest on public holidays because they afforded opportunities to gather with the church community. We designed our life and family schedule and holidays around big services, meetings, and demonstrating pastoral care for others. I do not deny that we had fun and loved being with our church family. We saw incredible transformations in others as they came to understand the person and salvation of Jesus Christ, and as our church grew exponentially, the pull of success was invigorating.

But I look at that public figure now and realise that God called her to something specific. Her story, her giftings and her ministry have led to incredible inroads in social justice around the world, bringing restoration, legislation change, and worldwide influence. Yet, the path God has her on is not my path. God did not create me so that I would be like her. Inspiring as she is, God has something specific for me, too. A big part of my ministry is how my husband and I choose to raise, love, and guide our children, encouraging them to pursue their individual callings and interests. Being entrenched in the busyness of ministry—distracted, tired, and striving—meant we were not giving our best to our children. Instead of receiving the most loving and patient versions of us, they had to settle for our leftovers.

God doesn't ask us to choose between our families and our ministry. Rather, God calls us to love. Paul reminds us in 1 Corinthians 13:1-4 that if we have incredible spiritual gifts, great faith, wisdom, and knowledge but don't operate in Christ's love, we are just a clanging cymbal and gain nothing. This passage of Scripture also provides us with a picture of love—it is patient and kind. It protects. It is not proud or self-seeking. It always hopes and always trusts. If our busy, tiring and distracted ministry lives are not leading us to live patient, kind and loving lives in our own homes, then it's probably time for a love audit. If our ministry lives mean we do not have time to connect with, love and encourage our spouses, we need to take a closer look at how God has called us to live. If our ministry lives are so busy that we do not have time to honour and cherish our parents, grandparents, or extended family, we are *too* busy. Oh, hindsight is a wonderful thing! Looking back, I see some of the ways we were not living out God's loving and patient kindness in our home despite living exciting ministry lives. Our kids came along for the ride, but it was our ride and not theirs.

I don't know what God has called you and your family to do. I don't know the ministry you are stepping into or those you may have stepped away from. I don't know the individual makeup of your family—their passions, interests, hobbies, and pursuits. What is important is that you know that, and God knows that. Working out God's plan for our lives is one of life's greatest adventures, made only more exciting (and complicated) by the introduction of spouses, children, and the myriad of family relationships woven into our lives. Yet, please remember that God has a plan for you *and* your family. You might have individual parts to play in His amazing plan, but God brought you together to outwork His purposes together. It requires give and take, compromise, humility, and servant-heartedness, but in the centre of His plan, there is love—patient, kind, humble, trustworthy love.

If you have children, speak with them about ministry decisions and listen to them and their hearts. Find out what makes them excited and what fills up their cup. Let them know they are loved and heard in your home. If you have a spouse, make decisions together. Treasure one another and create sacred, non-negotiable connection time away from your phones and emails. Pray together and champion the things God has placed on their heart whilst also stewarding the things He has placed on yours. If the ministry mission drives you apart, re-evaluate the mission. God has called us to live in unity and oneness with our spouse—He did not call one of us to run ahead and leave our families stumbling in our wake.

As part of our family's surrender and re-evaluation, we have been able to champion the activities our children are excited about. Sport plays a big part in their lives (that doesn't come from me!), and they find pleasure and contentment in challenging themselves in this area. They bring a voice to their teams that wasn't there before. Making time for friendship, musical instruments, and other ways to express their unique creativity has been a delight to us (even if we sometimes begrudge the never-ending sports practices, fees, and parent taxi-driving!). Giving them a say with regards to church, youth group, and our future in ministry has been insightful. Whilst we will always look to God first for direction and guidance, God gave them a voice too, and His Word instructs us that young people have an important part to play in God's plan (just look at Mary or King Josiah!). When your children know that you make time and space for them and are listening and interested in their opinions, it gives them a platform to speak what is in their hearts with honesty and trust.

Friend, your family is your first ministry, guided by God. They will be the ones holding your hand through sickness and health, good and bad. God put you together on purpose for a purpose—to work collectively and in unity towards all that He has planned for you. Championing self will lead to the crushing of another. Self-serving plans will only hinder the wonderful purposes God has for the family He has placed around you. Despite our shortcomings, God will work things out for good, but let's not get in His way. Let's lift up our spouses, children and parents in prayer and expectation. Let's love, support, and champion their ideas, creativity, and purposes. Let's sit with them, listen to them, encourage them, and discover with them. It may take time to reconnect with one another, but it is never too late.

# Spring Reflection

🌺 Consider the skills God has placed in your hand and the passions He has ignited in your heart. How do these skills and passions intersect to serve God and others?

_____

_____

_____

_____

_____

_____

_____

_____

_____

_____

🌺 Ask yourself if any of the things you are currently doing are distracting you from God's purpose and calling.

_____

_____

_____

_____

_____

_____

_____

_____

_____

_____

_____

❧ What are the messages your body is communicating to you in this season? How could you look after your physical body differently or better?

_____
_____
_____
_____
_____
_____
_____
_____
_____
_____

❧ Make a list of the activities that make you feel physically exhausted and those you might turn to as an 'escape' from physical or emotional pain. Do you notice any unhealthy patterns or coping strategies?

_____
_____
_____
_____
_____
_____
_____
_____
_____
_____

❧ Consider some of the things you love and admire about your immediate family. How can you champion your children/partner/ parents in their interests and God-given endeavours?

_____
_____
_____
_____
_____
_____
_____
_____
_____
_____
_____

❧ How might you better manage your emotions, time and energy to prioritise your family's needs and create an environment that enables them to flourish in this season?

_____
_____
_____
_____
_____
_____
_____
_____
_____
_____
_____

PART FOUR

# SUMMER

*Summer captures the early morning sun and the beauty of the evening sunrise. It is a gift earned through the loss, darkness and needed new growth of the seasons before. It marks the completion of a cycle, the joy and beauty holding a sense of triumph. Summer reflects a lightness of spirit that the previous seasons had not quite grasped. The memory of autumn and winter fade but are not lost. For it was autumn and winter that were necessary to usher in the growth and joy of spring and summer. Summer declares itself in full over the earth and sky, a promise of hope and of what is to come.*

# Summer: Restore

Amongst the rubble and debris
The ashen remains
Among the brokenness and fear
Something else has changed

Like a fresh green sprout
Breaking through the ground
A display of surprising colour
And emergence of a new sound

A deep knowing beneath
Anticipating dawn
Though the eyes only see desert
The deep awaits in awe

For underneath
And over time
The cracks start to give way
To a new cry

A cry of restoration
A cry of peace
As new life begins to wrap its arms around me

And suddenly
Like a symphony of change
A new season of growth
Begins to make its way

Through the dirt and grit and mess
The grace and hope of something new
Has once again
Broken through

# All Over Again

When the sunshine started pouring into our lives again, it was glorious. There were moments of joy where there had been none. There was laughter as the heaviness lifted. We began to have more fun in our home, and our eyes slowly lifted to the heavens as we allowed God to show us His goodness. God had already broken, uncovered and revealed, and now I was ready for Him to strengthen. Emotionally, I had become stronger. As God healed my heart, He brought people into my life who would champion me and give me space to grow and explore. I had room to breathe creativity into my work and the world around me. Activities that had been difficult in my season of pain became easier again. I once again welcomed the thought of meeting new people, serving in a church, communicating from a platform, and participating in the noisy chaos of family and community life. I had renewed energy, and the spark in my mind was reignited as the fog lifted.

Summer allowed me to reflect on the wonder of God's goodness and kindness. Acknowledging the mountains I had climbed and the valleys I had traversed, I could recognise God's handiwork woven through every moment of pain and learning. I had a newfound confidence in who I was, who God called me to be, and the gifts and passions He had placed inside me. I had established new rhythms to promote a healthier lifestyle, discovered deep and rich relationships, and identified important boundaries I needed to maintain.

Overall, I felt an overflowing sense of gratitude. I was thankful for all I had endured because of the purpose it held. I was thankful for the beautiful and stable relationships around me. I was thankful for God's grace that held and reassured me. I was thankful for my incredible family—always understanding, loving, and faithful. I was thankful for the person I was becoming, knowing full well the journey it had taken to get there. All over again, I recognised my overwhelming need for Christ. God had used the preceding seasons to help me carve out a deeper understanding of who He is, resulting in a greater reliance on and trust in His Word and a cavernous longing for His love and presence.

If I had the choice
I would choose this road again
Despite the mess
And despite the pain

You had to unfurl my closed-in spaces
You had to reach those unknown places

I would not go back
I choose this road I now travel
And all the fray I walked through

Knowing now
What I did not know then
That grace is sweeter
Love is deeper
That pain gives way to peace
Salvation echoing
Your fulfilment covers me

And the life I let you lead me to
Is far greater
Than what I could have imagined for myself

I'd choose you, and this, all over again.

# Trust Again

Trusting God with my life, my future and my purpose was an act of obedience—one that I deeply needed. I later came to understand just how fragile my trust in God and the work of the Holy Spirit in my life had become. Alongside my self-righteous thoughts and need for control sat a deep mistrust that God loved justice and would ultimately work all things out. I have an empathic heart, and the injustice I saw in the world was a load too heavy for me to bear. In ministry environments, privy to the realities of messy humans all around me, I frequently felt weighed down and heartbroken—even though I was a messy human myself. Whenever I witnessed a lack of integrity, selfish ambition, social injustices, or hurting humans, I felt compelled to find solutions and 'fix' all that was wrong in the church and the world. These 'Holy Spirit checks' initiated a reactive response in me that wanted to make everything and everyone okay.

As I began to question everything and dissect my theology, life experiences, and worldview, the burdens I carried became heavier, not lighter. It felt like rocks in my backpack. Every time I heard a story about injustice in the church, both locally and globally, another rock was added to my bag. When I reflected on some of my own experiences and allowed myself to feel the emotions of these experiences all over again, another weight was added. When another global conflict kicked off or when unnecessary poverty or greed continued to kill and destroy lives, yet more weight was placed upon my shoulders. These big rocks were addressed by my counsellors and confidants again and again. Over and over, I would hear that they were not my burdens to bear. These issues were almost always far outside of my influence or reach, and I was mostly helpless to instigate any change within the hearts of the people involved. When I tried and failed to address matters or shift an unhealthy pattern, I became frustrated, which led to stress. To me, it looked like too many vulnerable and hurt people, too many poor choices, and too much unnecessary pain. Prayer seemed empty and slow. I wanted justice *now*, and I needed everyone else to change to make it happen. I needed the world to stop hurting, and I did not trust God with this burden. I could not truly understand His grace and His timing, and I forgot that so much of who He is will always remain a mystery, that there were things about Him I may never understand or know.

I came to understand that the more I focused on other people's pain, ruminating on the hurt and searching for signs of injustice, the heavier my backpack became. Wrapped up in trying to determine the 'right' theology to prove someone wrong (even if it was just in my mind), I wandered down the deep, dark rabbit hole of abuse within the church. No matter what environment I found myself in, my propensity towards justice weighed me down. Anger and frustration impacted my mind, body and emotions, creating barriers to meaningful relationships and developing in me a hardened, cynical mindset.

Don't get me wrong, I am very aware that God is the God of justice. As Christ's followers, we are encouraged "to act justly, to love faithfulness and to walk humbly with [our] God" (Micah 6:8 HCSB). Amos describes God's heart for justice as a rolling river, more important than our fancy offerings and displays of public worship. But I did not trust God to take care of injustice, war, human trafficking, dishonesty, or moral failure in His church because I could not see Him working. I was happy to accept His forgiveness and mercy in my own life and feel justified. But I could not fathom how God could extend this same grace to those around me—especially those who had hurt others. Although the Bible is full of stories of redemption, when God extended His merciful hand to someone undeserving, I struggled to accept the reality of this when I saw and heard of it happening. I found it difficult to engage in this grey area between grace and boundaries, redemption and justice, and God-given authority and the abuse of power. So, I kept carrying the burdens with me, hoping that justice would eventually prevail.

It wasn't until I felt ready to reconnect with and serve God through a church community that I realised the power these thoughts still had over me. I still didn't fully trust God—or other people. Even in the context of a healthy environment, I continued to hold onto mistrust, fear, and other people's hurt. These thoughts went beyond sound wisdom and discernment, beyond healthy boundaries. They went beyond having a servant's heart and a love for people. And they left me in a place of emptiness.

I needed to accept that God held all of my cares in His hand and that He cared about the things that troubled me and occupied my thoughts. I had to trust that justice would flow like a river—whether I lived to see it or not, in this world or the next. I could not continue to sit in the brokenness of others and allow the anger of injustice to constantly torment me. I knew God had created me with a heart for justice, which had opened doors for me, led me to some amazing places, and drove me to love and care for others wholeheartedly. It motivated me to serve others, live generously, use my words to uplift others, and be a light in the darkness. But I needed to draw the line between what God had called me to do and that which I needed to entrust back to Him—which was a lot.

When I started to exert more self-control over my thoughts and allowed God to bring peace about certain situations and people, I felt the burdens lift. I was not gaslighting myself—my concerns were real, and the injustices were heartbreaking. But I stopped myself from ruminating over situations and overplaying scenarios in my mind that triggered my heartbreak and anxiety. I prayed about the issues I had influence over and even harder about the ones I didn't. I starved any conversations or thought processes that fostered bitterness or unforgiveness, and my husband (thanks, babe!) became good at redirecting me when I started to spiral down the same winding path again. I became more aware of the things I did and did not have control over. I began to trust the God of justice to do what He says He will do in His Word—in His way and in His timing. I had to go through a process of rewiring some of the thought processes that I had developed, being conscious of my emotions towards something or someone, and putting boundaries in place regarding the content I watched and the voices I listened to. This did not mean I was ignorant or naïve to the hurt, abuse or heartbreak of others or that I was turning a blind eye. My compassionate heart would never allow me to do that. Instead, I stopped these burdens from dictating the posture of my heart and the state of my emotions. I allowed myself to lament without trying to fix and control the things I couldn't. And it freed me. It freed my heart to be able to heal, to process emotion in a healthy way, and to move forward with trust and hope.

Throughout this season of burnout, I also lost trust in myself. I started doubting everything I thought I knew and had heard from the Holy Spirit, no longer sure what was real or imagined. Struggling to discern wisdom, I began unpacking decisions I had made and wondering who I was really listening to. When we place others on a pedestal and that pedestal tips, it can shake us to our core, undermining the foundations we have built for ourselves. Amid the fallout, I remember vividly standing in the middle of a church conference, crying out to God. I just wanted to hear His voice. At that moment, I strongly felt God's reassurance, and it broke me. I had no doubt He was reassuring me that I knew Him, I could hear Him, and I had indeed heard His voice again and again throughout my journey. All of those heart checks I had experienced along the way when things just didn't sit right, all those times my body had communicated to me through exhaustion, pain, and emotion—it *was* the Holy Spirit speaking, and I *had* heard Him. I didn't always follow His promptings, and I didn't always agree or choose to listen. But rather than condemning me, He kindly and gently encouraged me that I could trust His voice. This reassurance renewed my confidence and strengthened me as I shared with others the ways the Holy Spirit had guided and helped me. And when I felt a tug in my soul about something, raising questions or suspicions, I did not ignore them or dismiss them as cynical or negative thoughts. Instead, I chose to be curious and share them with God, allowing the Holy Spirit to thresh out my thoughts, fears, concerns, or misguided judgments in the knowledge I could fully trust His Word and wisdom.

The emotional pain I experienced and witnessed within the church context also left a residue of distrust. The church as a whole, which had once felt like a sanctuary to me, had become a source of questioning and cynicism. This breakdown had been subtle throughout my journey—the full impact of it was not recognisable until I began entering these rooms again. But my desire for hope and healing persisted. Trust was elusive as I navigated relationships in new spaces and faced familiar expectations and intentions. Yet, I asked God to reveal Himself to me in the hearts of others and to place trustworthy people in my midst. As I navigated these steps, slowly and cautiously at first, I had a greater sense of God's wisdom.

One of the first steps in this restoration process was gaining a new understanding of trust—not blind or unquestioning but rooted in discernment and wisdom. God gave me a clearer lens through which to see my relationships, helping me to distinguish between healthy and unhealthy dynamics and expectations. Instead of placing people on pedestals, I began to have a more balanced view, recognising we are all flawed individuals with the capacity to be instruments of God's love and grace. I approached new team environments and church connections not with naïve optimism but with grounded faith and a sense of God's presence with me. I was able to see that trusting others did not mean ignoring red flags or bypassing accountability but trusting that God, in His wisdom, would guide me through each relationship. I did not feel that same sense of pressure to be and do everything the way I had in the past; rather, I had a choice about how and when to engage.

God also began revealing the intricate and purposeful ways He had created those around me, giving me a clearer vision of His goodness within them. He helped me to view people through His eyes, seeing beyond the outward expressions—all the traits that might have irked me in the past—to the inward intentions of their hearts. With God's help, I was able to explore and determine what was personality or preference as opposed to power, control, or arrogance. God brought the understanding that every community is messy, complicated, and full of humans who make mistakes, are dealing with internal battles, and whose personalities, though different to mine, all represent the creativity of God. Though I am still more guarded than I used to be, my heart is now more open to others, more confident in who I am, and more able to see beyond my own hurt to the needs of others.

Friend, I pray that the Holy Spirit continues to reveal Himself to you and that you would discern and hear Him. I pray that you will continue to trust His voice and direction in your life—even when you doubt and are unsure. His still, small voice might just be a whisper, but I encourage you to listen to it and trust that you are hearing Him. I pray that as you navigate your personal journey, God will give you the wisdom and compassion to reestablish stable, trustworthy, loving relationships in your life and allow you to see, with a clearer vision, the community you have around you to love and lean on.

# In the 'Sift'

In my summer season of re-engagement, I had to trust that God would lead me to the right places and people. Earlier seasons had included a lot of sifting, shedding, and subsequent isolation. Unhealthy thought patterns, anger, control, anxiety, perfection and unhelpful relationships were being removed from my life. Threshing the wheat had led me down a path of pain and discovery, and I had let go of a lot. But in this next season, I came to a point of re-entry. The chaff had blown away in the wind—the superfluous processes, unhealthy expectations, perfectionism, and need for control—and the valuable kernels of wheat had been collected. On the ground, however, some kernels remained. These represented the things I had surrendered for a season that God was now asking me to pick back up. The hardest thing was deciding what was wheat and what was chaff.

In the sift, God reminded me that the things I had laid down were not all regrettable. There were the sweet connections we had made throughout our journey, the laughter as we served together, the excitement and energy we shared as we worshipped, and the amazing changes we witnessed in hearts and families. Initially, I wanted to forget it all, sweep it under the carpet and leave it in the 'too hard' basket, but this was just hurt and bitterness speaking. When I read through my journals from those times, I am reminded of many beautiful and memorable moments—acts of immense generosity, great celebration, the awe of what God was doing. And the deep love we felt for those we served with never waned. In the book of Ruth, we see that during harvest season, Boaz would leave some of the wheat in the field so that someone in need might pick it up as he went by and be blessed by it. (This was something God had instructed the Israelite people to do in Leviticus nineteen.) Likewise, I felt the need to walk through the field again and take another look at what I had left behind. God knew I had needed to lay everything down in order to heal, but now He was prompting me to take another look, through the lens of healing, wholeness, and wisdom.

With my bent towards justice, I had carried so much anger about things that were happening in the global church, including financial mismanagement, moral failures, celebrity culture, and business models taking priority over discipleship and pastoral care. Sometimes, it made me want to ditch my Christian faith completely as I wondered what kind of light we were putting out into the world. Incredible stories about the underground church in Iran or spiritual uprisings in third-world communities seemed far removed from our comfortable Westernised churches. We had so much at our fingertips and sacrificed so little in comparison. Yet, when I brought this burden to God, He helped me see that re-engaging with the church wasn't an all-or-nothing decision for me. As I slowly sifted through the chaff, God allowed me to see the grain.

Whilst I still erected many boundaries and allowed myself some hesitation as I re-engaged with church life, I also chose to see the generosity and kindness in the people I met. I chose to hear a gentle word, an encouragement from one believer to another, and a call to discipleship and learning. I chose to see the positive impact of God's people on local communities at a time when so many families were struggling. I chose to see honest and pure hearts worshipping God together in auditoriums. I chose to raise my voice once again in worship, singing songs of praise that brought joy and fulfilment. I chose a posture of learning and openness rather than cynicism and anger. I chose to believe again in faith, trusting that God was in the midst of any and every situation and would move if and when He wanted to. Looking past the imperfections I was trained to focus on and fix, I could more easily see the joy in imperfect community, humble leadership, sound biblical knowledge, and generosity towards one another. I believe God placed me in environments that brought out the best of these things, and, in doing so, He opened my eyes to His goodness within the context of the church.

This summer season gave me the capacity to see things differently and exercise choice about where I felt God was leading me and what He had placed on my heart to do. It allowed me to engage slowly and with intentionality, creating space for consideration, conversation, and questioning. My confidence may have improved, but I was still on a journey of strengthening and renewal. I had a choice about what I picked back up again. This meant that within the church environment, I took time to determine what was valuable both to me and to God. I took time to separate the wheat from the chaff. I asked questions. I chose to let some things go and pick others up. I chose to trust community again and the people whom God had placed around me. I chose to be vulnerable when the time was right. I chose to see God even when I felt triggered and let Him guide me through the threshing process, however painful.

Friend, you might be in a season of threshing. Perhaps you are still disengaged and not yet ready to inspect the grains lying on the floor. Maybe you are at the point of re-engagement, wondering where to start. Can I encourage you to take it slow? Take your concerns, frustrations and triggers to God, and let Him guide you in this sifting journey. Remove what is unhelpful, but open your eyes to see the value in people, places, and past experiences. Allow God to show you a safe and compassionate community that will bring soul-filling relationships to your life once again. God is with you in the sifting—trust Him.

# Oh! The Joy

Joy and creativity were some of the first things to disappear from my life when I was depleted, but it has been invigorating to see them return in my summer season. I almost felt surprised when I began laughing out loud again—belly laughing! God has brought some wonderful people into my life who understand my Kiwi-English humour and make me laugh until I almost wet my pants. (I have three kids and a weak bladder, so this could happen at any time!) Deep thinkers like me really need these people in our lives to help us lighten up, be present, and enjoy the moment.

Music is another agent of healing for me, and I began to find joy again in worship and song. I remember a student in high school once asking me if I was okay. When I asked him why, he replied he had not heard me humming and singing to myself as I typically did every day on the way to school. Singing has always been such a big part of my life— an extension of my personality and thought processes. I had songs for various moods, for healing, for gratitude, for worship, for fun, and definitely for dancing. I remember driving to work during my autumn and winter seasons with the same songs on repeat—songs about faith, healing, finding peace amid brokenness, and those that cried out for change. The words were an elixir for my soul, and in moments of tearful surrender, I would feel peace and courage. I skipped the songs that triggered me and leaned into a newfound appreciation for diversity in music and song. I used those seasons to discover new music and sounds, which acted as a balm for my mind. These included instrumental worship and soaking music (William Augusto has been my favourite artist), sounds of rain to help me sleep, and upbeat praise music to keep rhythm as I walked. As spring turned to summer, I felt my passion reignite.

As I travelled with God on this inward journey, I also discovered other things that brought true joy within me. Whilst I had always viewed myself as an extrovert, someone who was energised through connection,

I found that solitude also brought an immense sense of peace and joy. I'm still not clear whether this shift was a necessary part of my healing journey, but I came to relish quiet, independent moments more than I ever had before. Even writing this book has been a process of quiet joy for me as I carved out the space to reflect and express my thoughts. I began to set aside time to bask in nature, walk along the beach, try new things, read for fun, and speak with God in prayer. Although time with others still energised me, I found that intentional solitude revitalised my heart, mind, and energy, leading me to greater joy, fulfilment, and rest.

Walking has been a source of joy for me on many days. I love early mornings full of fresh air and awe as I look upon trees, clouds, and birds, and I appreciate the privilege of walking safely alone in my neighbourhood. When I can, I go to the ocean or into the bush around local hills and walking tracks. In my winter season, I began walking every day before work. This usually meant a 4:45 a.m. wakeup, and early nights, yet it was a small price to pay for the benefits it offered my mind and body. Walking is something I always come back to, even if I am no longer as consistent as I used to be. It allows me to spend time with God. It also helps to clear my head, and the endorphins that flow through me when I move my body trigger positive emotions within me.

Living in Australia, I am frequently accompanied by incredible birdsong, but my ultimate favourite is the cry of the black cockatoo. Considered an elusive bird in this area, it comes and goes with the seasons and is not a common sight. Not long after moving here, I discovered that black cockatoos frequent the area at certain times of the year, and it has been my mission over the years to see as many as I can. Every time we hear their recognisable call in the sky, my kids yell out to me, "Mum, your birds!" and I come running outside to watch them fly overhead. In the stillness of the morning, I have been awed to see flocks of them perched in the trees close to my walking path. The joy I feel in these moments when I come across my favourite birds, only God will know.

Sometimes, amongst the big things
Outside of my control
I need to look at the small

A hot cup of tea
A fresh morning walk
The sound of dusk birdsong

A game of cards
Freshly baked scones
An affectionate child
With a hug and kiss

Pen and paper
And the simplicity of a smile
In a world of more and plenty

A deep breath of clean air
A candlelit bath
And a well-weathered book

A hot shower
And fresh sheets
Bedtime stories and evening prayers

These pockets of hope seem small
But somehow significant
They are fleeting
But they matter much

Throughout this journey, I realised how much I need an outlet for creativity to bring me joy, as without it, I feel stunted and stuck. Although my life lacked creativity for a season or two, especially in autumn and winter, I have been able to get my creative juices flowing again through personal pursuits (like writing this book!), participating in projects in my workplace, and getting reconnected to a church community. I realise God gave me the capacity to come up with novel ideas and concepts, find creative solutions, and put thoughts and ideas into action. Creative projects bring me great joy, light a spark in my brain, and help me connect with God. Yet, creativity is one of the first things to go when I am exhausted, feeling low, or on the precipice of an autumn season once more. When I no longer have the energy for writing, creating, or generating new ideas, this is my cue to stop, rest, and reset.

Friend, God is a restorer. He restored the joy I had always carried but with a depth I had not experienced before. So, let me encourage you that the sun will come out, and joy will return. (I speak this in faith for you also.) And when it does, it is so sweet. My joy returned as I discovered new relationships and treasured old ones, saw my children grow and mature, worshipped in a room with others, and found my voice again. I do not take any of these moments for granted, as I know what it takes to get here and how hard the journey can be. So, I encourage you to find joy in the small things if you are struggling with the bigger picture. Treasure rain on the window, a cosy cup of tea, birdsong, a bubble bath, your child's laughter. Spend time with your crazy, fun friends, and let them take you out for a drive in the sun, even if you don't feel like it. Notice when your joy is waning and take a moment to stop and rest. My prayer for you is that God would restore your joy in new and surprising ways, like He did for me, and that He would help you experience small joys, even amid hard circumstances.

# When to Say 'No'

Whilst much of my writing has reflected on my personal journey, I do feel the need to say something about the abuse faced by those in a church ministry environment. In writing a book about pain and burnout, I can't possibly shy away from the stories I have been both saddened and privileged to hear concerning abusive behaviour behind the closed doors of church meeting rooms, backstage green rooms, and people's homes. I know many people who have experienced deep hurt and trauma from verbal, spiritual, emotional and even physical or sexual abuse within a ministry environment. As a woman of faith and also a social worker, I need to reiterate that abuse in any environment is not okay. Let me be clear: it is not godly. It is not justifiable or excusable. I understand that it can be easy to get caught up in the idol of ministry and ignore or justify behaviours because the markers of success are good. People are coming to know Jesus. The church is growing. You might have charismatic and successful leaders who are loved and revered. They might have a public platform and be people of influence. They might be strong at a time when you are vulnerable or searching. There are many ways this plays out, but there are no circumstances in which abuse, coercion or manipulation are acceptable.

We need only to look back at God's commandments to love God and love others (Matthew 22:37-39). We must return to 1 Corinthians 13, which talks about love being patient, kind, and trustworthy. James tells us we should be slow to speak, slow to anger, and quick to listen (James 1:19). He later warns us that our words have power and it isn't good to praise God whilst also cursing people made in God's likeness. Fresh water and salt water cannot flow from the same spring (James 3:9-11). God also calls us to look after the poor and humble, not favour the rich and well-known. In Proverbs 11:3 (NIV), we read, "The integrity of the upright guides them but the unfaithful are destroyed by their duplicity." A life of honesty, honour, and reliability—both in and out of the spotlight, on a platform, and behind closed doors—will guide our ministry leaders, but those who choose duplicity will eventually be undone.

If you are led by those who speak and act differently behind closed doors, I urge you to guard your heart and attend to the Holy Spirit's promptings within you. Listen to His voice and test what you see and hear against God's lovingkindness. If you know of things happening in the darkness that need to be brought into the light, speak up. Perhaps your leaders do not take accountability, acknowledge poor behaviour, or accept the guidance and discipleship of mature leaders. Maybe you have spoken of your concerns and have been shut down, gaslit, cut off, or discredited. If that has been your experience, I urge you to seek wise counsel outside of that leadership circle. It does not matter how successful someone is. It does not matter how many people are walking through the door of the church. It does not matter how unqualified or inexperienced you might be. If you have been a recipient of behaviour that would be reportable to authorities in any other environment, please do the same. The church should be a safe haven, and abuse is never justifiable.

1 Timothy 3 tells us that to be a leader in the church is an honourable thing and carries much responsibility—leaders should be above reproach, sober-minded, respectable, hospitable, and self-controlled. They should be gentle, not a lover of money, able to teach, not a drunkard, and not argumentative. There are a lot of expectations listed here! This sometimes means we place judgment and high expectations on the shoulders of our leaders. If you are a ministry leader or pastor, you will inevitably feel the weight of responsibility for the pastoral care, salvation and growth of your flock, and it can be difficult to carry. But remember, you are not alone, and it is never too late to introduce accountability into your journey. Surround yourself with people you can be vulnerable and honest with, and permit them to question you. Invite them to speak up. Ask your team how they feel when you walk into the room and how you are perceived. Don't be fearful of their criticism; be open to wisdom and reflection. Allow yourself to be discipled by people you trust and glean the wisdom of those who have gone before.

In this life, there will be trouble—we know this all too well. Sometimes, we make poor choices, and people get hurt because of it. If you have hurt people or treated them badly, own it, speak up, and get help. If you are struggling with sin behind closed doors, move past your shame and shed light on it by talking to someone. It won't go away by itself. God is a miracle maker, and He can do the impossible. But God also created us to live in community and embrace the vulnerability that community brings. Proverbs 27:17 reminds us that iron sharpens iron, so go and find some iron. Take time to heal if you need it. Be humble with those you've hurt. Be honest about your shortcomings. If you have abused others, now is the time to acknowledge it to others and let justice be done through the appropriate channels. It's never too late, and there is no sin out of God's reach.

The way we treat others, the sin we keep behind closed doors, and the darkness that spills from our lips or through our actions are often symptoms and reflections of our inward chaos: insecurity masked in arrogance, shame masked in success, fear masked in perfectionism, the inner workings of our personal histories leaking out onto others. We do certain things and act in ways to protect ourselves from the story that lies beneath. Yet, God is aware of your history and your struggle. Being open and truthful about your past with God and trusted confidants does not make you weak. Rather, the vulnerability of your heart opens doors that lead to change. Trying to pretend everything is great and successful and strong whilst your inner world is falling apart actually invites distrust from others and exhaustion for you. If you are a church leader or pastor, ensure that you deal with your inner world. You cannot pour life into others from an empty vessel, and you can only uphold a false sense of self for so long before the cracks start to show and the people you lead lose their confidence in you. Allowing God to work through the pain leads to restoration and learning that becomes the foundation for stronger relationships, trustworthy leadership, and a wholeness that only He can provide. This is hard and heartbreaking work at times, but it is so necessary for yourself and others.

If you have been the recipient of abuse within the church, I lament with you. It is a burden too heavy for you to carry. I pray that light will be shed on your situation and that justice will be done. Please report abuse through the right channels, including the police where relevant. I am sorry that people have let you down, betrayed you, or abused you. I pray that amid your pain, God will show you His love, gentleness, and compassion, just as He showed me. I pray that God would reveal to you His true nature, far removed from the abuse and power of others, and you would be able to lean into His healing and experience the restoration only He can bring.

I know without a shadow of a doubt that God sees you. The moment you were a mere thought to God, you held incredible value. You are worthy, you have purpose, and you have a place in God's faith community. So, if you are hurting, angry, or indifferent, He will wait. And while He waits, He will love you with wild abandon. Wherever you are, He is with you. And though I do not understand the mysterious ways of God, His timing, or His plan, I have great faith that there will be justice—whether we see it in this life or the next. Until then, I pray for peace and restoration for your soul. *Selah*.

# Forever Learning

In every season, there is learning. It does not stop. When things are going well and life is good, we tend to either lean into God's goodness or insist that we're the ones guiding the steering wheel. If we don't stay alert and aligned, we can easily revert to unhealthy patterns, habits, and ways of thinking. I had to learn that God's desire for me to S L O W down was not just a passing phase; it was an invitation into a new way of life. I didn't just get back up after a while, brush myself off, and keep going. Rather, I needed to maintain my newly formed routines because the learning I have done in this last season is a form of preparation for every other season to come. I now know what saps my energy. I know what reinvigorates me. I know my preferred sleep cycle. And I know the habits, thought patterns and distractions that could so easily ensnare me once again.

I have discovered over the last few years that my body has a lot of muscle memory; it keeps the score. In the early stages of recovery, it would easily tip over the edge into pain and sleeplessness. As time passed and my body, mind, and spirit became stronger, I reached that point less and less. But on occasions when I reverted to old habits and patterns—the frenetic schedules, late-night Netflix to numb my mind and distract from stress, poor sleep, and a reduction in exercise which impacts my brain function and mood—I paid for it. Even after we have established new patterns of learning, our minds and bodies do not erase the old ones so easily, and we can quickly end up back to where we started—exhausted and broken. It is our responsibility to practice self-control and discernment to ensure we make wise decisions that benefit our souls, our minds, and our bodies. Yes, there will still be life events, unexpected circumstances, and trauma that we do not have control over. But when it's possible to do so, we need to be ready to put our 'big girl' panties on and make wise, mature decisions again and again and again.

Although summer was primarily a season of maintaining health and routines, it also brought new learning and reflections. I have learned that if we lean in during painful seasons, we can always find something new to learn, understand, or meditate on. It could be a deeper understanding of God's compassionate love for us; understanding our history, family and genetic disposition with greater clarity; or learning how to forgive, how to heal, or how to trust God and His Word. During my summer season, I had to rethink and rearrange how I did things, especially relating to my marriage and family life. I needed to keep learning to understand my psyche, my history, and my unique personality and temperament. In this season, I challenged myself to try new things (like jumping out of a plane!) and stepped out of my comfort zone, no longer bound by fear. I was adamant that I would continue to live with purpose, and I did not want the residue of my pain to hold me back from the possibilities in front of me.

Amid this season of learning, life went on. I continued to face unexpected events, experience disappointment, conflict and pain, and see those I love walk through similar challenges. It was important for me to realise that walking through a hard season did not exempt me from the fallibility of humanity. I was human, after all, and would continue to navigate this joyous, messy, exciting, mysterious, wonderful, unpredictable thing called life. Summer was not void of hard things, but it brought a new perspective and enabled me to grapple with them differently.

This season also brought a restoration of mind and spirit, which invigorated me and allowed me to move forward in wholeness. I experienced first-hand how God takes the broken and shattered pieces of our lives and puts them together to form something beautiful. It reminds me of the Japanese art of Kintsugi, where cracks are repaired with traces of gold to create a masterpiece that is far more beautiful than the original. Let's imagine a Master Potter who spends time, effort and love creating something He is proud of, something He wants to present to the world—that's us. We amaze and thrill Him with our individuality, creativity, and unique design. But as we weather storms, moves, and breakages, we become cracked, broken, and imperfect. Now imagine that same Potter, picking us back up off the shelf and lovingly, carefully pouring His 'gold' into the cracks that have appeared over time. This is intricate work—He is not just designing something new but creating something more beautiful out of broken pieces. Instead of simply hiding the scars that appear on the surface, He weaves beauty and healing through the cracks, creating a beautiful masterpiece out of our imperfections. The design is still there. The original blueprint is still visible. But those weathered storms and breakages combined with the beauty of the gold form something even more magnificent.

I remember talking through this process with my counsellor, understanding more about myself, my personality, and the gifts God had uniquely placed inside of me. At that time, I could not imagine ever being the person I once was. I was too broken. But the seed had been sown, planting words of truth in my spirit about who God had created me to be. Truth has a way of cutting through the brokenness and piercing our hearts. It sparked feelings of hope and joy for my future and the realisation that my broken pieces were not the end of my story. God was still working, still repairing, still creating.

And so it is with all of us.

Ephesians 2:10 tells us that we are God's workmanship or masterpiece, created on purpose to do the works He has planned for us. Amid the repair, He still has plans. Amid our brokenness, we still have a purpose.

God does not discard us when we remain imperfect or walk with a blemish. He is so kind to continue weaving His truth and healing through our scarred, broken pieces. As this truth is revealed, we have a new and unique capacity to outwork His plans in ways we couldn't before, our lives reflecting His workmanship. At any point, we can surrender to the Potter and allow Him to do His work within us, to weave truth through our scars. The result is breathtaking—it is healing, it is renewal, and it is restoration. He creates a mosaic of truth and life within us that allows us to continue His work and fulfil our unique purpose. Our journey is never wasted, friends. He creates. He heals. He restores. He replenishes and renews. He will create a masterpiece from our broken pieces!

Like a beautiful mosaic
Pottery woven with gold
You paint a picture of value
Uniting the new with the old

As I look at the reflection
I see you in my story
In moments of fear and pain
You were with me again and again

In moments of despair
Where desolation seemed to win
I now see your gracious hand
Weaving gold from within

And in the end
The beauty you pour into this broken heart
Has healed the wounds
A journey of wholeness
That resembles the finest of art

# Summer Reflection

🌹 Identify any barriers or triggers in your current season that might stop you from engaging with your faith community.

_____

_____

_____

_____

_____

_____

_____

_____

_____

_____

_____

🌹 Consider if any of your current activities sap your energy or emotional capacity. How might you create effective boundaries to protect your physical and mental health?

_____

_____

_____

_____

_____

_____

_____

_____

_____

_____

_____

🌹 Reflect on any healthy habits or patterns that have helped you in the past. How could you make permanent space for them in your daily routine?

_____

_____

_____

_____

_____

_____

_____

_____

_____

_____

🌹 Who are the people in your life you can trust to help you bring any hidden darkness, shame or trauma into the light? What is stopping you from reaching out?

_____

_____

_____

_____

_____

_____

_____

_____

_____

_____

✿ Make a note of what you are learning as you walk through this season with God.

_____

_____

_____

_____

_____

_____

_____

_____

_____

_____

_____

_____

# Epilogue

As I sit here in the early months of 2025 and reflect on my journey and the process of writing this book, I am in awe of God's kindness, His gentle reassurance, and His constant presence. There were times when I wondered how I could ever move forward and walk through the pain, yet it has been a therapeutic process, allowing me to write, reflect, share, heal, and grow. My journey evolved from an incredible inconvenience and debilitating experience to a restorative and insightful pilgrimage.

Over these last few years, I have had to take responsibility for my emotions, my reactions, and my thinking. I have learned to adjust my expectations of others and, even more so, my expectations of myself. It has been necessary for me to maintain healthy patterns and rhythms. Since I was living in such a frenetic way for so long, it is tempting for me to glide back into those patterns if I do not stay intentional and alert. There have been times of busyness or stress when rising cortisol levels began to impact me again, but my new-found awareness and learning caused me to quickly pivot and make changes to protect my health.

The anxiety that introduced itself to me for the first time during this journey still pops up from time to time, prompting further reflection and requiring me to make further adjustments. I have walked through uncomfortable things with purpose despite my anxious feelings, knowing that the absence of discomfort (in a safe environment) does not help me to learn and grow. These moments of reflection become monuments of change, and the learning we take from these seasons leads us to be stronger in the next. It takes time and sometimes many steps backwards. This is not to minimise the experiences of those living with persistent and debilitating anxiety. It is essential that we extend deep and unwavering love for anyone (ourselves included) who is navigating mental health challenges. I recognise and support those walking this path and understand the profound impact it can have on our lives.

I find myself in a place of openness in this season: open to the leading of the Holy Spirit, open to others, open to future hopes and dreams, and open to further learning. Though it is not all smooth sailing, I know who I am now, and I can stand firm on what I know to be true about God. I still get triggered in the church environment, and I cannot say that I have answered all my questions, removed all my concerns and doubts, or reconciled all that has been broken. I am still a work in progress. But while God continues to lay out a path before me, I choose to trust His voice in me as I abide in Him. I choose to trust steadfast and faithful friends, humble and loving leaders, and wise confidants. No matter what steps I take to improve my spiritual, emotional and physical health, I find I am most at peace when I just abide quietly in God's presence and trust Him. Only He can bring the soul-filling, satisfying rest and peace that I crave.

I have, at times, wrestled with shame as I considered sharing my weaknesses, my poor decision-making, and my health setbacks in this book. Somewhere deep inside, there is still the seed of doubt that being open and honest with others holds value. Even now, it takes courage to be vulnerable and open myself up to the reactions of others, wondering if my weaknesses and difficult experiences somehow disqualify me in their eyes. I have realised, however, that I am the person I am because of this journey I have travelled, and sharing it with others has created deeper bonds, opened doors, and sparked curiosity in others. I hope that sharing my journey will, in turn, inspire you to share yours, creating an interconnected story of learning, wisdom and insight that impacts all of our lives.

This book was originally titled 'Pockets of Hope'. Despite every unexpected turn, dark valley and the pain I have endured, I have been able to find pockets of hope along the way. I even have a tattoo on my forearm to remind me of this truth. I now live with greater insight about myself, greater understanding of God and His love for me and others, and a deeper need for His grace and presence in my life. I have come to know that people are the greatest treasure. No success, accolade, lifestyle or goal is more important than the people God has placed on this earth. They bear a treasure far greater than we can fathom in our hearts—the image of God. We were created in all of our intricacies to bear the image of Christ here on earth, each one of us a new and exciting representation of His creativity, love, and goodness. If you are a leader or pastor, the greatest privilege you have is looking after your flock, introducing them to our God, and showing them how loved they are by Him. We should, therefore, hold people in high esteem—above growth statistics, above perfect services, above our online image and preaching roster—for they are a reflection of God Himself.

If you have read through my journey and found yourself nodding in agreement, crying in recognition, or standing in solidarity, I am grateful. This book is as much for you as it has been for me—a journey marked by healing and knowledge and change. I pray that it has encouraged and blessed you, maybe challenged you, and hopefully softened and opened your heart towards our loving God. I pray your reflections contain Holy Spirit-inspired insight that gently challenges and leads you to the inner work that God is calling you to do to prepare you for upcoming seasons. I have changed as I have written, and written as I have changed. I am grateful for the person I am now, the obstacles I have overcome, and the maturity God has shaped within me. I continue to hold a deep love for all those we have journeyed with. Ultimately, I am so grateful that I can share this journey with you.

*In every season,* God was with me. *In every season,* there were pockets of hope. *In every season,* I was loved. *In every season,* I found community. And *in every season to come,* I know that He will walk beside me in truth and wonderful, wild love.

# Acknowledgements

**To my husband, Tumanako.** You do not know how much you carried me through this process. You saw me at my lowest, supporting me, holding me up, filling every gap I was suddenly unable to fill. You have offered unwavering strength and encouragement in ways no one else will ever understand. I have come to understand more fully how much I need you in my life. You are a fantastic and present Papa to our kids, always fun, active, attentive. I can't wait for all of our future adventures!

**To my beautiful children, Tia, Ariel and Atlas.** You may not fully know (until you read this book) what I have journeyed through, but you remember how things were for me, you saw Papa supporting me, and you all have been an incredible source of joy and strength. I love the continuing learning journey we are on as parents and am constantly in awe of the people you are becoming and the creativity God used to create each of you. I love you all more than you know.

**To my parents.** Thank you for being a source of love, support and wisdom for me always and for encouraging me to seek God through this whole process. You laid a sturdy foundation of faith for me and I am so grateful. You have championed this writing project from the beginning, excited about every step along the way. Thank you for affirming me with confidence and faith.

**To my dearest Emily.** You are as solid as a rock. I trust you fully and know that I can come to you with anything. Thank you for being my sounding board, for being truthful with me and encouraging me to keep going when I wanted to give up. You never turn away from a challenge, you're not afraid of my hard questions, and you have been with me and for me through this whole journey. I thank God for you constantly!

**To Rach Un.** You are consistent, faithful and trustworthy. Thank you for letting me ugly cry over the phone, express my hurt, pain or grief and thank you for always being there for me. The depth of our friendship has multiplied greatly because you allow honest conversation, nothing is off-limits, and I can be myself with you. We have been through a lot together, and I'm grateful to have a lifetime friend in you.

**To Ray Andrews.** What a gift you are to the Christian community. Early on, you spoke life and truth to me and helped me to unscramble my thoughts and emotions, bringing wisdom and revelation. Your encouragement and advice provided enough confidence in me to step into the unknown challenge ahead of me.

**To Yvette.** I really appreciate your honesty, wisdom and theological insight. Thank you for reading and giving me feedback on my initial manuscript and helping me to shape the direction of this final copy. I am grateful to have you in my world and look forward to more nature walks, intense discussions and sharing in the messiness of family life and parenting.

**To my work colleagues**—Justin, Ange, Jo, Jess, Gabby, Grace, Elyssa, Kerry, Kristal. I came to you when life was messy and you provided me with a compassionate, loving, grace-filled work environment with loads of fun, laughter, and friendship. Being able to pray with colleagues, to disagree and debate safely and to have a place where I can breathe creativity in my work again has been so life-giving. You have helped me to build confidence again in the person God designed me to be. You have allowed me to try new things and take risks and have played a huge role in my healing and restoration, even though you probably did not realise it.

**To Anya McKee and the team at Torn Curtain Publishing.** Thank you for believing in me, a rookie with no idea what I am doing. I came to you with a concept and a story whilst I was still healing. You helped me to refine and form this project as it took shape, determining what the Christian community needed and encouraging me to be as vulnerable and real as possible. This has been a wonderful learning experience for me, and I am grateful you took a chance on me!

To my Naturopath, **Elizabeth Orme** and my Professional Supervisor/ Psychologist, **Phil Slade**. Thank you for helping me to understand my physical body and my mind in a way that is gentle and honest and helps me to understand and grow.

**To everyone else** who has been a part of my journey, whether in large ways or small. Thank you for connecting with me as we have crossed paths, for impacting me in some way, for offering friendship, wisdom, possibly tears, challenge and most likely big hugs. You all form part of this mosaic God has created, and you are the gold that is woven through my journey.

# About the Author

Rachel Rerekura-Tamaiva was born in Wellington, Aotearoa New Zealand, moving to Australia with her husband and children in 2013 to support friends in the pioneering of a new church. A trained social worker (BSW Hons), Rachel has worked in disability services, university accommodation, youth justice, and the education sector. Rachel is passionate about social justice issues. She has travelled to Cambodia twice to learn about human trafficking and support non-profit organisations working in the area. Rachel has participated in A21 marches and led fundraising events for organisations working with vulnerable women and children. She has a deep yearning within her to see all Christians engaged in supporting and loving 'the least of these' and bringing heaven to earth for those in need.

A born adventurer, Rachel enjoys trying new things, including skydiving in 2023. She loves to visit new places and learn about different cultural groups, immersing herself in the culture and the people she meets. In her visits to Cambodia she has enthusiastically eaten fried crickets, barbequed frogs legs, and crocodile—just some of the delicious local cuisine!

Rachel enjoyed writing from an early age including poetry from the age of ten. Encouragement from teachers led her to a constant flow of personal journaling and poetry and later in life, an interest in creative writing projects such as design, media and script writing in the church ministry context.

Rachel and her family were heavily involved as leaders, staff members and as volunteers in their church in Australia. When her health declined in 2020, the urge to write felt heaven-sent, enabling Rachel to express what was happening spiritually, emotionally and physically. Today, she writes with wisdom, humility and a sense of vulnerability about the realities of her journey through burnout. Her greatest desire is that others will find healing, grace and hope as they process their own ministry and life stories.

Rachel is married to Tumanako and they have three children together, Tia, Ariel and Atlas plus two children lost to miscarriage. They live on the Gold Coast, Australia.

To get in touch with Rachel or for speaking requests, please email:
**info.rachelrt@gmail.com**

Follow Rachel on Instagram **@rachel_rerekuratamaiva**
or visit her website:

**www.rachelrt.com**